THE JUGGLER'S GUIDE TO

Managing Multiple Projects

THE JUGGLER'S GUIDE TO

Managing Multiple Projects

MICHAEL S. DOBSON

PROJECT MANAGEMENT INSTITUTE

Library of Congress Cataloging-in-Publication Data

Dobson, Michael Singer.
    The juggler's guide to managing multiple project / by Michael S.
Dobson
        p.   cm.
    Includes bibliographical references (p.   ).
    ISBN: 1-880410-65-6 (pbk. : alk. paper)
    1. Industrial project management.   2. Time management.   I. Title.
HD69.P75D628   1999
658.4'04 – – dc21   99–13074
                                            CIP

ISBN: 1-880410-65-6

Published by: Project Management Institute, Inc.
              Four Campus Boulevard
              Newtown Square, Pennsylvania 19073-3299 USA
              Phone: 610-356-4600 or Visit our website: www.pmi.org

TABLE OF CONTENTS

FIGURES

ACKNOWLEDGMENTS

This book is dedicated to my nieces and nephews:

Van Patrick Martin

Samuel Franklin Dobson

Sarah Frances Dobson

Gary Harlan Grisham III

Carolyn Ann King

and my honorary nephew:

Justin Michael King

SECTION 1

Introduction

CHAPTER 1

The Art of Juggling

You may remember an act from the old Ed Sullivan show where a man takes a plate, balances it on the end of a long pole, and gives it a spin. Then he repeats the process with another plate, then another, and another until there are about eight plates spinning. During the rest of the act the man runs from pole to pole, shaking the poles carefully in turn to keep the plates spinning. The plate spinner is always just a second away from disaster.

That is what it means to juggle multiple projects. Normally, the study of project management focuses on managing a single project. Most available material on *multiple projects* focuses instead on time management and priority setting. These are vital skills. In fact, if you do not develop good time management and priority-setting skills, you will not be able to put the tools in this book to good use.

Now, assume you know how to set priorities, put first things first, organize work-space, and do all the other things you are supposed to do. After all that, you are still juggling seventeen different projects. All are important; all are job responsibilities; all have high payoff; and you start to feel like the drowning victim going down for the third time.

If you manage multiple projects, you are no stranger to stress. You may feel like the plate spinner just described. Frequently, multiple project managers end up working extra hours, feeling overloaded, and sometimes failing to achieve their goals.

There is a strategy that goes beyond time management and the basics of formal project management. It shows how to take multiple projects, put them on a timeline, determine resource requirements, handle emergencies, and put you in charge of your work, possibly for the first time in your life.

This concept is called *portfolio management. The Juggler's Guide to Managing Multiple Projects* teaches how to apply this concept to an individual situation.

DEFINITIONS

Before moving on, examine these key definitions.

A *project* is a specific work assignment outside the normal job routine that has a planned end and a measurable accomplishment to achieve.

Work is the rest of the job to be accomplished while juggling projects. Work has no planned end to it.

A *portfolio* refers to a collection of projects comanaged under the same management umbrella.

When different people talk about managing multiple projects, they often mean different things. Meet three multiple project managers with very different situations and problems. Then explore their situations in more detail, and learn how the concept of *portfolio management* can work for them.

TASK-ORIENTED PROJECT PORTFOLIO

Task-oriented projects are relatively small in amount of work and time. Each project might take hours, or at most a day or two, if you could handle it in an uninterrupted fashion. That is not the case, however. Task-oriented projects are challenging because they are often numerous and because the person responsible already has a regular job to do full time.

Carolyn is the human resources manager for a thirty-person company. A one-person department, she's responsible for benefits administration, payroll, compliance with federal and state regulations, hiring, records management, training administration, and personnel policy. She's supposed to be available to consult with managers and supervisors on personnel matters, to help employees with the full range of human resource (including personal) issues, to report regularly to senior management, and to keep her department functioning smoothly. Right now, she's working sixty-to-seventy-hour weeks just to keep current. She needs an assistant, but that is not likely in the current financial climate.

This is a sampling of her current project list.
- *Find a new health insurance carrier; the existing one just raised rates.*
- *Arrange computer skills training for six new administrative assistants.*
- *Coordinate with accounting to streamline the current payroll system.*
- *Develop a new employee newsletter and management feedback program.*

INDEPENDENT PROJECT PORTFOLIO

Independent project portfolios consist of projects that are not directly connected to one another. If one should fail (or succeed beyond expectations), it does not greatly affect the other projects in the portfolio. The challenge in managing independent project portfolios is that resources (people, tools, equipment, money) available to complete portfolios are normally at a fixed level. Planning and allocating those resources becomes easier when you use the right techniques.

Patrick is the publications director for a national trade association. The trade association publishes a monthly magazine for industry professionals, a quarterly journal of research data, annual industry surveys, highly technical management books, annual meeting volumes, and a variety of brochures and one-shot publications. He manages a staff of two writer/editors, one graphics designer, and two desktop publishing technicians.

Because the work his unit does is so different from the other work of the trade association, he has a difficult time explaining the demands put on his unit.

These are some of the issues that concern him.

■ *The authors of his books and many of his articles are industry professionals, not writers. Sometimes their work requires heavy editing in order to be readable.*

■ *His authors are frequently late with their manuscripts, but he cannot miss his deadlines. This results in unplanned overtime and rush charges at the printer.*

■ *A variety of special projects, such as marketing brochures and tradeshow books, are assigned to his department at the last minute, further disrupting his schedule.*

■ *He'd like to have his department take better advantage of new technology to streamline the editorial and publishing processes, but he can't find the time for training and conversion in his already packed schedule.*

INTERDEPENDENT PROJECT PORTFOLIO

Interdependent project portfolios are large projects in themselves. Many of the tasks in the large project are so complex and time consuming that they are essentially projects in their own right. In an independent portfolio, the projects are not connected to each other; however, in an interdependent portfolio, they are very connected. The success of the entire portfolio depends upon the successful accomplishment of all the projects within it. The interdependent project portfolio includes both the issues of an independent portfolio and some special issues of its own.

Sarah manages the data processing center for a 300-person insurance company. With twenty staff members to supervise, a large mainframe computer, network file servers, a new Internet site, hundreds of personal computers throughout the company, and daily special project requests for new reports and service, it's a demanding job. Sarah is on top of it, and her department has a well-earned reputation for quality.

The company has experienced remarkable growth over the past few years, so much so that it has now outgrown its old facility. It will be moving into a brand new facility in the next year. Sarah, in addition to her regular responsibilities, must coordinate the move of the computer center, a highly complex activity with the possibility of disaster if something major goes wrong. Since the move is going to happen anyway, Sarah thinks this might also be a good opportunity to upgrade the ten-year-old mainframe computer and internal network.

The move into the new building involves a number of projects that all fit together.

- *Create a backup strategy for all files and software to guarantee that no records will be lost.*
- *Develop and implement a strategy to ensure that critical computer services are not interrupted during the move.*
- *Plan and manage the physical move of the electronic components.*
- *Plan and manage the move of the rest of the center.*
- *Coordinate the purchase of new equipment and arrange for installation.*
- *Arrange training for all affected staff.*
- *Prepare manuals and documentation for the new system.*

Which one of these three people—Carolyn, Patrick, or Sarah—has problems most similar to yours? ("All three at the same time" is a legitimate answer.) You will learn how to manage each of the three types of project portfolios in this book. The exercise on the next page will help you discover what type of portfolio you have, so you may concentrate on those chapters that will be most helpful to you.

What Type of Project Portfolio Do You Have?

1. **Start by listing several of your multiple projects below. You do not need to be exhaustive at this point.**

   _____

   _____

   _____

   _____

2. **Approximately how long would it take to complete an average project assuming you could ignore everything else and focus on it?**

   _____ Less than a day (probably task oriented)

   _____ Less than a week (task or independent)

   _____ Less than a month (independent)

   _____ Less than six months (independent or interdependent)

   _____ More than half a year (probably interdependent)

3. **Approximately what portion of your day is required to complete your normal activities, and what portion is available for project work?**

   _____ Normal work takes essentially 100 percent of my time, and project work is supposed to be done on top of it (probably task oriented).

   _____ Normal work takes 40 to 60 percent of the day, project work, the remainder (task or independent).

   _____ Normal work takes 10 to 30 percent of the day, project work, the remainder (probably independent).

   _____ Virtually all my work is project work; normal activities are a minor part of my day (independent or interdependent).

4. **My projects are primarily small one-shot activities.**

   TRUE   Probably task oriented

   FALSE   Independent or interdependent

5. **My project is extremely large and is an out-of-the-ordinary situation for me.**

   TRUE   Probably interdependent

   FALSE   Independent or task oriented

6. **The various projects in my portfolio are not primarily connected to each other, even though they may use the same resources to get accomplished.**

   TRUE   Task oriented or independent

   FALSE   Probably interdependent

SECTION 2

Task-Oriented Project Portfolios

CHAPTER 2

Juggling the Task-Oriented Project Portfolio

"What makes my projects so tough?" Carolyn asks. "Several reasons come to mind.

"First, my regular job is a full-time job. Handling human resources issues for thirty people takes time.

"Second, my days are filled with emergencies and unplanned events. Somebody's having a problem working with a boss, or a subordinate, or a coworker. There's an important meeting, and a few of the issues may affect human resources, so I need to be there.

"Third, many of my projects don't have deadlines. I get so wrapped up in immediate problems that I lack time to get to important long-range issues—until they turn into crises.

"Fourth, all my jobs seem to have Priority #1. It's vital that we get some new health insurance for the staff. It's vital that we straighten out the payroll problems. It's vital that we improve employee communication.

"Fifth, well … I'm generally a very organized person, but with everything I'm supposed to do, it's easy to let details slip through the cracks."

DEFINITIONS

Here are some key terms you will want to become familiar with as you explore task-oriented project portfolios.

A *project* is an assignment with a measurable goal and limited time and resources available to accomplish it.

A *task* is an assignment with a measurable goal and limited time and resources available to accomplish it.

The difference between a project and a task is *perspective*. Many people think of a project as the whole work and a task as part of a project. However, a small project can be a single task. A large project can have tasks within it so large that those tasks are projects in their own right.

A *task-oriented project portfolio* is a portfolio of small projects, each consisting of a small number of tasks. Each project in the portfolio is treated as a single task to help schedule and manage the work.

The projects in the task-oriented project portfolio are generally small. If it were not for the number of them, and for the regular work that has to be accomplished, these tasks would be a minor problem.

Professional project management concepts usually are not applied to simple tasks, to avoid overkill. The tasks do not need that level of technique to manage them effectively. However, when task-oriented small projects pile up, you will benefit from using selected project management concepts.

A FOUR-STEP TECHNIQUE FOR MANAGING THE TASK-ORIENTED PROJECT PORTFOLIO

Task-oriented portfolio management takes time-management techniques to the next level. It assumes you already know basic concepts of time management and have managed to apply at least some of them in your work.

Step 1: Establish a Project Control System

When projects come irregularly and frequently on top of your regular work, you need an effective mechanism to keep track of them. One powerful option is to design a *project control worksheet*. You can create your own, or use the version provided in Figure 2.1.

Properly managing each of your projects includes making sure you have all the data organized and accessible. Take your time to do this right. By drawing together all the information you need into a single place, you gain the ability to prioritize, look realistically at your productivity requirements, and control more easily the performance of the work.

The project control worksheet shows the information you need to gather on each project. Do not feel restricted by the size of the form, or feel obligated to fill it. The amount of information you need necessarily varies by the type of project and project conditions.

Project:	

Project: _____

Priority: _____

(I × U = S) _____

Importance: _____ **Urgency:** _____

Comments: _____

Who assigned: _____ **Date assigned:** _____

Specifications/Deliverables:

- _____
- _____
- _____

Resources-People/Department:

- _____

Equipment/Supplies:

- _____

TIme Estimate: _____

Person-Time: _____ **Calendar Deadline:** _____

Milestones:

- _____
- _____

Cost Estimate:

$ _____

Figure 2.1 Project Control Worksheet

You must answer these questions about the project.

- Who is going to do each project (if not you)?
- How long will each project take (total work and calendar time)?
- How much will the project cost (use of resources as well as actual dollar)?
- What are the deliverables and outcomes of the project? (What does it have to do?)
- What is the relative priority of the project (in relation to everything else you must do?)

To use this system, complete a project control worksheet as soon as you are assigned any project. You may not have all the information at the outset. If you do not, complete what you can and know you will have to gather the rest of the information before you can begin work.

Keep your project control worksheets together in a file, so you can track your total project load at any time. Later you will learn how to use calendaring techniques to move from the project control worksheet to the work of your project.

Prioritizing (and Reprioritizing as Needed) Your Projects

One of the differences between the plate spinning act and real life is that, in the act, all the plates have equal value, but, in real life, some plates are fine china and others merely melamine. If you cannot keep all the plates in the air, let the melamine drop. You cannot manage multiple projects successfully unless you prioritize them correctly.

A powerful formula for priority management is:

$$I \times U = S$$

In this formula, you assign a number (usually from one to three, with one being the highest) for how *important* (I) the work is. Assign another number (also from one to three, with one being the highest) for how *urgent* (U) the work is. Multiply the numbers together to get the *success* (S) rating, which will be between one and nine. The lowest success ratings confirm your highest priorities.

Measuring Importance

Your multiple projects have differing degrees of importance. Importance is a measure of value, of payoff.

One method of deciding the level of importance is to imagine that you do not do the project. What would be different if you chose not to do it at all? What benefits would you lose? What are the negative results? If little is affected by not doing the project, it is not important.

What is important also depends on your goals. The same projects are not important to everyone.

Follow these steps to effective goal setting (see Figure 2.2).
1. Establish a mission.
2. Define your goals.
3. Set your objectives.
4. Plan your activities.
5. Measure the results.

Mission. First, your mission dictates what is important. Why are you in business? Why does your department exist? Why are you here? Missions can be organizational, departmental, individual, and personal.

Goals. Effective goals come from well-defined missions. What are the most important steps to take to help achieve or advance a mission? Goals and projects are never ends in themselves, only means to an end. If you achieve the wrong goal, and achieve it brilliantly, you still have failed. Why does Carolyn need to research a new health insurance carrier? It

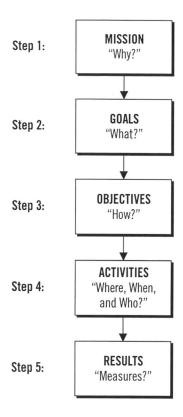

Figure 2.2 Five Steps to Effective Goal Setting

might be to save money, or it might be to increase coverage for employees, or it might be to eliminate certain restrictions, or it might to replace the current carrier who is refusing to renew coverage. The goal will determine Carolyn's ultimate strategy.

Objectives. Objectives are the specific criteria assigned to the goal to measure progress. Depending on the reason Carolyn needs to find new health insurance coverage, she may establish different criteria for her search, change her deadline to accomplish the goal, and change the priority of this project compared with others.

Activities. Activities are the action steps in the project. What exactly must be done? What are the interim and final deadlines? Who will complete each portion of the project?

Results. The payoff of the project comes if accomplishing it made progress toward your mission. If Carolyn's goal is to save money with the new carrier, she can measure whether she succeeded. If Carolyn is trying to increase the coverage offered to staff, she can measure whether she succeeded.

Measuring Urgency

Multiple projects have differing degrees of urgency (U). Urgency is a measure of time pressure.

One method of deciding the level of urgency is to imagine postponing the project until after its official deadline. What would be different? What benefits would you forego? What are the consequences of not meeting the deadline?

While urgency is significant in organizations, *urgency addiction* is detrimental. That is what happens when people get too focused on time pressure and not involved enough with value. For example, some people who go through college seem to learn one lesson: when to start writing term papers. If the lesson is "wait until the night before," and you carry that habit into the workplace, you may suffer from urgency addiction. Do you tell people, "I work best under pressure?" If you do not have enough crises in your life, do you create some?

Urgency stimulates the body's production of adrenaline. Adrenaline is a drug, as is speed or cocaine. People can become dependent on the rush, the excitement of going all out to meet a deadline.

Successful project professionals need to move beyond urgency addiction. Pre-planning and good organization reduce urgency.

Legitimate urgency factors are part of good project planning. If there is a reason why now is better than later, do it now. Avoid unnecessary urgency. The best way is to head off problems before they get out of hand.

Rank the urgency of a project as follows:

- Urgent 1 = Today or sooner!
- Urgent 2 = Soon, within a week or two.
- Urgent 3 = Flexible, can fit into schedule.

Urgency alone is a poor indicator of priority. Many things are urgent—if you do not do them today, you lose the option to do them at all—but they are not important.

For example, every single telephone call is urgent. If you do not pick up that receiver when the telephone rings, you will not talk to that caller at that time. Only a handful of calls are important.

Many important things are not urgent. *When* you take a seminar does not help you get a promotion, but you will not get the promotion until you take that seminar. The seminar is important (it has value) but not urgent (there is no time pressure). Make sure you prioritize your tasks, considering both importance and urgency. In the event of a tie, choose the more important task. Use the *Project/Goal Planning Worksheet* in Figure 2.3 to determine the importance and urgency of your tasks; then prioritize them.

Step 3: Determine Available Time and Resources

Carolyn has both a full-time job to do and multiple projects that she must somehow fit into her schedule. While a management professional is no stranger to overtime, she must examine causes, cures, and options if overtime is an uncontrollable and regular part of her life.

PROJECT/GOAL PLANNING WORKSHEET

Top Three Priorities for:	I × U = S			$^1 2_3$

Priority Description and Deadline	Purpose — Why?
1	
2	
3	

Figure 2.3   Project/Goal Planning Worksheet

Virtually every book and seminar on time management and organization recommends that you keep a time log (see Figure 2.4) for a few weeks to measure how you are spending your time. Many times, lives are filled with time wasters you do not even recognize. One rule for self-improvement is if you do not know you have a problem, it is hard to motivate yourself to fix it. You may be amazed at how much you can increase your productivity once you discover how you are wasting your time.

After you have kept the time log for at least a week (preferably two weeks), add up how you are spending your time. You may find some real surprises.

Do not feel inadequate if you have some entries under *personal business* or *chatting/gossiping*. Face it. No one is 100 percent focused and on target all the time. Several management books suggest that a productive employee works fifty minutes in each hour, with ten minutes for relaxing, chatting, personal calls, and going to the bathroom. If your nonwork items are within the ten-minute-per-hour range, do not worry.

If, on the other hand, you are wasting three hours a day in nonproductive business and you have to work overtime hours each day to keep current, cut some of the time wasters to reduce the amount of overtime you are putting in, and still accomplish all the work.

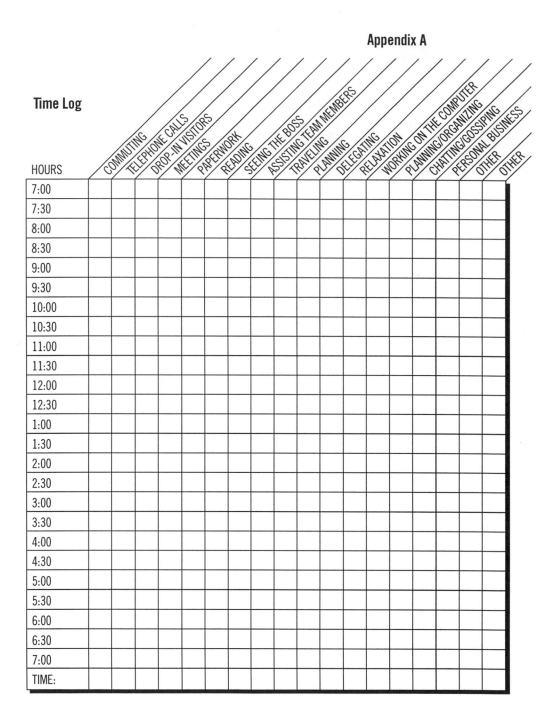

Figure 2.4   Daily Time Log

Look also for time wasters in the job. Are your telephone calls coming so frequently that you cannot get five uninterrupted minutes to think? Are people always camped on your doorstep waiting to see you? Are you trapped in endless meetings? Good time-management books and seminars offer strategies for coping with on-the-job productivity killers. Get them under control so that you will be able to focus on your own high-payoff activities.

The value in doing steps one through three is that they organize you and encourage your thinking about the projects you have to do and scheduling them into the regular day. Even when you have analyzed your work and controlled your time wasters, your workday will still consist of three categories:

■ regular duties
■ crisis management and problem solving
■ strategic reserve time.

Regular duties. A significant part of your time log will be devoted to your regular duties. These are ongoing nonproject activities. You need to figure what part of your workweek is consumed with taking care of regular duties. If the percentage is too high (It can be 100 percent!), you need to strategize ways to make it possible to perform project-related work.

To find more time for projects, remember that within regular duties there are priorities. Some regular duties may need to be postponed, delegated, or even dropped to make time for project work.

Regular duties can be subdivided into *time-fixed* and *time-flexible* duties. Scheduled meetings are time-fixed, as is the production of the weekly report. Work that needs to be done but can be shifted within a day or week to help organize priorities is time-flexible.

Crisis management and problem-solving time. Good project management skills reduce the number of crises in your job, but they do not eliminate crises entirely. For the average professional, between 40 and 60 percent of the workday is uncontrollable. Carolyn must deal with walk-in visitors, randomly occurring personnel problems, and a variety of daily issues that cannot be scheduled in advance. Based on your time-log, figure out what percentage of your workweek is taken up by these unforeseen and uncontrollable situations.

Again, if the percentage is too high to allow enough project time, you can take the following steps. For a two-week period, write down all the different emergencies that land on your desk. Now examine them for common causes.

If, for example, Carolyn spends three hours over two weeks helping people interpret their health insurance plans, then it is clear that the contract conditions are confusing. A summary memorandum clearing up confusing points, a briefing on health insurance procedures for all staff, or setting office hours to address health insurance problems would reduce or even eliminate this time-draining situation. Many problems happen because there is an underlying situation. If the underlying situation is fixed, those problems will go away.

How do you find the time? You must, even if it requires overtime on a one-shot basis. A famous office cartoon reads, "When you're up to your rear-end in alligators, it's hard to remember your original objective was to drain the swamp!"

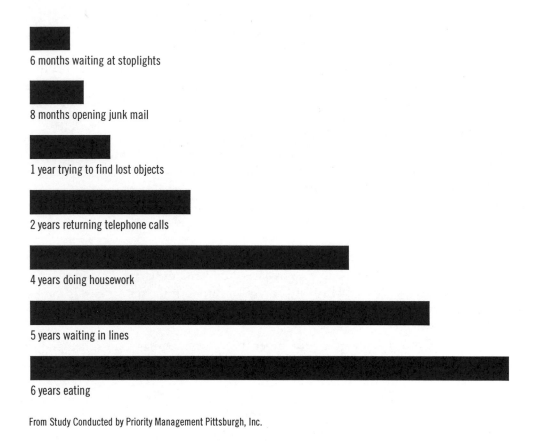

6 months waiting at stoplights

8 months opening junk mail

1 year trying to find lost objects

2 years returning telephone calls

4 years doing housework

5 years waiting in lines

6 years eating

From Study Conducted by Priority Management Pittsburgh, Inc.

Figure 2.5   How We Spend Our Time

You cannot afford to forget your objective. If your work is overloading you, you must take steps to uncover the causes of the overload. Otherwise you are condemned to stay in your current situation.

Strategic reserve time (SRT). SRT is what you have once you have budgeted for regular duties, crisis management, and problem solving. It is the only opportunity you have for project work and for cleaning up some of the underlying situations that currently plague you. Follow the time-management strategies described to maximize your SRT. Then you can allocate time to complete your projects and improve your work.

Step 4: Put Your Projects in Your Calendar—and Do Them

What if you end up with an hour or two each day of SRT? That is quite a lot of time if you know the *law of the slight edge.*

Imagine you are in a car on the interstate. The car next to you is going only fifty-four miles per hour. You want to pass the car, but you cannot go faster than fifty-five. That is frustrating. You feel you are creeping as you pass; yet, in only one hour, you are an entire mile ahead.

Imagine you have only an hour a day of SRT. It does not seem like much time. What real difference can you make in your life in a single hour?

What if you spend an hour a day, seven days a week (count your personal goals along with your professional goals), working on long-range projects that lead to improvement in your situation?

In one year, you will spend 365 hours. At eight hours per working day, that is a little over forty-five working days. That is over two months at a rate of twenty working days per month. This is the law of the slight edge.

Two months. Imagine you have the next two months completely free to work on projects, both professional and personal, which would make a difference. Where would you be in a year?

Break your projects into tasks. If your SRT is an hour or two a day, you have five to ten hours a week of project time. You need to break each project into action steps, each step an hour or so in length. Schedule them into your calendar.

For this purpose, it is appropriate to take a weekly or monthly approach, rather than a daily approach, to calendar your tasks. You may have some days with so many meetings and regular assignments that it is hopeless to plan any project work. Other days are much lighter in regular work, and you have more time available for project activities.

Use the *Planning Your Priorities Worksheet* (see Figure 2.6) to break each project into action steps.

Put the tasks in your calendar. Every professional needs a calendar management system. It can be a large wall calendar, a daily planner or organizer, or a computer software program (if your work keeps you primarily at your desk and your computer can be on all the time).

Tip! To stay organized, use one calendar and use it to schedule everything, both professional and personal, in your life.

Look at Carolyn's schedule for May. After keeping a time log for three weeks, she discovers several things she can do to maximize her SRT. After she takes all the steps available to her, she finds that her regular work, including paperwork, meetings, filing, and so on, absorbs about three hours of her day. Problem solving, responding to others, takes up nearly 50 percent of her schedule, totaling four hours per day. That is seven out of eight hours committed. On average, she has an hour each day, or five hours each week, of SRT.

In the month of May, Carolyn therefore has twenty-three hours of project time. After reviewing her projects, she selects the three projects with the highest priority and schedules them first: 1) Buy a new health insurance policy; 2) Start upgrading the payroll system (since accounting and data processing departments will have to do most of the work); and, 3) Arrange for computer skills training for the new administrative assistants.

Using a *Project/Goal Planning Worksheet* (see Figure 2.7), Carolyn lists and prioritizes her projects. On the form, she also does the breakdown of steps for the first of her projects.

Now, it is time to put the projects on her calendar. The monthly calendar overview from Carolyn's personal organizer is shown in Figure 2.8.

PLANNING YOUR PRIORITIES

I × U = S	Project:		
	Description:		
		Deadline:	
Purpose:			
Action Steps:		Deadlines:	✔

Figure 2.6   Planning Your Priorities Worksheet

PROJECT/GOAL PLANNING WORKSHEET

Top Three Priorities for: May 1996	I	× U	= S	1 2 3
Health Insurance Policy	1	2	2	1
Payroll Upgrade	2	2	4	3
Computer Skills Training	2	1	2	2

Priority Description and Deadline	Purpose — Why?
1 Health Insurance Policy — New Carrier 5/31/96	Current one raised rates need to get lowest cost for same coverage
2 Payroll Upgrade — Coordinate w/Accounting & ADP (By June or July)	Time/cost saving project for long-range benefits
3 Computer Skills Training for Admin. Assts. (ASAP!)	Need new admin. assts. to know WordPerfect and Excel for Windows.

	Action Steps:	Deadlines:	✔
1	Health Insurance Policy		
Set up meeting w/ ins. agent (10 min.)		5/1/96	✔
Have mtg. w/ agent (90 min.)		5/7/96	✔
Receive brochures/info (10 min.)		5/10/96	✔
Review brochures (3 hrs.)		5/15/96	
Decide on carrier (1 hr.)		5/16/96	
Meet w/CFO on decision (90 min.)		5/17/96	
Meet w/Agent on decision (60 min.)		5/21/96	

Figure 2.7   Project/Goal Planning Worksheet

MAY 1996

Sunday	Monday	Tuesday	Wednesday	Thursday	Friday	Saturday
			1 HEALTH INSURANCE: Call agent for appointment Timesheets to payroll	**2** 1:00 PM Personnel Meeting COMPUTER SKILLS: Review training companies	**3** NEWSLETTER: Write/send memo to employees for input	
5	**6** PAYROLL UPGRADE: Call Accountant to set up meeting	**7** 11:00 AM HEALTH INSURANCE: Agent appointment	**8** NEWSLETTER: Compile employee feedback Timesheets to payroll	**9** 1:00 PM Personnel Meeting COMPUTER SKILLS: Review training companies	**10** COMPUTER SKILLS: Call Vendors for prices (1 hr.)	11
12	**13** 1:30 PM Grievance Hearing—R. Smith HEALTH INSURANCE: Review brochures (1 hr.)	**14** HEALTH INSURANCE: Review brochures (1 hr.)	**15** HEALTH INSURANCE: Review brochures (1 hr.) Timesheets to payroll	**16** 1:00 PM Personnel Meeting HEALTH INSURANCE: – Call agent for appointment – Decide on carrier (1 hr.)	**17** 11:00 AM HEALTH INSURANCE: Meet with CFO on policy	18
19	**20** 10:00 AM PAYROLL UPGRADE: Meet with ADP manager COMPUTER SKILLS: Make vendor decision	**21** 1:30 PM HEALTH INSURANCE: Appointment with agent on decision	**22** COMPUTER SKILLS: Schedule training for staff Timesheets to payroll	**23** 1:00 PM Personnel Meeting NEWSLETTER: Prepare sample for Executive Committee	**24**	25
26	**27** 3:00 PM NEWSLETTER: Meet with Executive Committee	**28**	**29** Timesheets to payroll	**30** 1:00 PM Personnel Meeting	**31** Monthly report	

APRIL 1996
1 2 3 4 5 6
7 8 9 10 11 12 13
14 15 16 17 18 19 20
21 22 23 24 25 26 27
28 29 30

JUNE 1996
1
2 3 4 5 6 7 8
9 10 11 12 13 14 15
16 17 18 19 20 21 22
23 24 25 26 27 28 29
30

Figure 2.8   Sample Monthly Calendar Showing Time Allotted for Projects

Carolyn first schedules her repetitive work tasks, including the weekly preparation of payroll timesheets each Wednesday, the weekly personnel meeting each Thursday, and the end-of-month report. She also schedules one of the problem-solving issues, a grievance hearing on Monday, May 13. (Her daily schedules will list other regular duties as they arise.)

Carolyn knows that her month will contain emergencies for which she has not yet planned, so she wants to leave herself a reasonable margin to avoid overload. You will notice that she schedules most of her project related activities for days early in the month. Currently, she does not have any project work scheduled after May 28. That allows a safety margin if the project work takes longer than expected or if emergencies exceed expectations for the month. If she does not need the safety margin, she will use the time to start her next projects.

One task for the health insurance project is to review all the brochures and contracts of the different policies. Carolyn estimates it will take her about three hours to do this. Since her SRT is an hour a day, she spreads this work over three days (May 13–15) and makes her final decision on the fourth day (May 16).

Carolyn now has a working schedule for the month. It is an ambitious amount of work but, with a good plan, she will succeed.

Verify task completion. One of the psychological advantages of breaking your projects into bite-sized tasks is that it becomes much easier to do each part. It feels more manageable; you feel more productive.

Now, Carolyn needs to focus each day and each week on accomplishing her scheduled work. She needs to verify that she has met deadlines and completed her work.

After a few months' experience with the new system, Carolyn feels far more in control of her work. She says:

Look, it's still difficult. I have a demanding job and a lot to do. But once my tasks are planned and in my schedule, I don't have to keep worrying about these huge items looming over my head. I can take it one day at a time, one project at a time, and get it done.

Complete Your Own Project Priority and Planning Worksheets

1. Start by listing the current projects for which you are responsible.

Project	Description	Deadline	Purpose—Why?	I × U = S

2. **Take the top three priorities based on your I x U = S ratings and complete the Project/Goal Planning Worksheet.**

PROJECT/GOAL PLANNING WORKSHEET

Top Three Priorities for:	I × U = S			$^{1}2_{3}$

Priority Description and Deadline	Purpose — Why?
1	
2	
3	

3. For your top-priority project, complete the Planning Your Priorities Worksheet, listing action steps (in one-hour segments) and deadlines.

PLANNING YOUR PRIORITIES WORKSHEET

$I \times U = S$	Project:		
	Description:		
		Deadline:	
Purpose:			
Action Steps:		Deadlines:	✔

4. Put each in your calendar—and get at least one project accomplished this month.

SECTION 3

Independent Project Portfolios

CHAPTER 3

Juggling the Independent Project Portfolio

"Everything I do is a project," Patrick says. "At any given moment, I'm managing between five and ten simultaneous projects. I complete over fifty projects each year—all with a tiny staff, under tough conditions, and with a lot of uncontrollable events, such as getting manuscripts from people who have the knowledge but not the writing skill."

Patrick's office and the small work area for his publishing team are normally buried in a sea of paper. Manuscripts, galley proofs, paste-ups, and printing contracts show the large number of projects going on. A metal scheduling board highlights key deadlines and issues, but Patrick says it's more honored in the breach than in the observance.

Everyone on the team works hard—very hard. In spite of everything, deadlines slip. Patrick wants to get control, to get the work out without punishing his staff every working day.

"I'm ready to try anything," he says.

DEFINITIONS

You will need to understand these key terms before proceeding.

An *independent project* is a project that is part of a portfolio of projects, usually similar in subject matter, for which success and failure is independent of other projects in the portfolio.

Cross-project resources are the people and tools that accomplish the projects in an independent project portfolio. While the projects do not directly relate to each other, they draw on the same resources. If a resource is late on one project, it can affect the next project for which the resource is scheduled.

Projects in an independent project portfolio typically involve similar subject matter. Patrick's projects are all in the publishing area: books, magazines, and reference guides. Some projects may be outside the primary subject area. For example, Patrick might have a project to upgrade desktop publishing hardware and software or develop more freelance editorial support to handle production logjams. Although the subjects of these projects differ, they are all related to the core business of publishing.

Patrick's situation is not wholly different from Carolyn's. Like Carolyn, Patrick has regular management duties, meetings to attend, special assignments from the boss, and other activities that take up part of his day. Similarly, his staff has regular duties.

When thinking about managing an independent project portfolio, remember that the techniques described in the next few chapters are *in addition to*, not instead of, the techniques for managing the task-oriented portfolio.

Independent portfolio projects may be of any length; typically, they are more substantial in size, length, scope, and complexity than those in a task-oriented portfolio. Each project will take weeks of work with a dedicated team to complete even if nothing else is being done in that department.

SINGLE PROJECT MANAGEMENT VERSUS MULTIPLE PROJECT MANAGEMENT

Because of the difference in project size, if you manage an independent project portfolio, you can benefit from the techniques of professional project management.

A definition you learned in Chapter 2 allows you to use single project management techniques on multiple projects:

Project = Task

The words *project* and *task* are synonyms—the practical difference is perspective. As a result, you can use single project management techniques on multiple projects as long as you treat each project in your portfolio as a task on the charts.

You will learn exactly how to do this step by step. First you need to learn single project management techniques.

CHAPTER 4

Planning a Single Project

Patrick is responsible for publishing a monthly magazine for industry professionals. The magazine contains articles on new developments by industry companies. Freelance journalists write articles and supply photographs. In addition, the president writes a monthly column (which is always late), and the executive director writes another. Every issue requires a cover and cover story that focuses on one key person in the industry. The magazine also contains advertising from member companies and by organizations that supply products and services to the industry. The back of the magazine contains regular display ads and a classified section.

The deadline for each issue allows little flexibility. To reach members during the first full week of a month, the issue has to be mailed the last week of the previous month. Printing takes six days. Therefore, the May issue must be at the printer the last full week of April. All editorial, design, and production work must be completed, all approvals from management obtained, and the complete package turned over to the printer by that date.

That is one issue of one magazine.

First plan this single project, then learn how to combine it with others to make a multiple project schedule.

DEFINITIONS

The *triple constraints* are the three components of a project definition: how much time you have, how much money or resources you can use, and what the project must accomplish. Usually these three parts are called time constraint, budget constraint, and performance criteria.

The *driver* is the most important of the project's triple constraints. The other two constraints are ranked as *middle* and *weak*.

The *work breakdown structure* (WBS) is a method for breaking your project into component tasks and organizing the management structure.

Network planning is the process of putting the project's tasks in the order they need to be done. You may put your tasks in a *dependent* or *parallel* sequence. The *network diagram* is also called a PERT chart or CPM chart.

Task analysis is the process of gathering together all the information you need to manage each task in your project. It is a great aid in delegating.

A *Gantt chart* is a timeline chart that shows the sequence of tasks in your project over a calendar period.

THE TRIPLE CONSTRAINTS

Baseball great Yogi Berra once observed, "If you don't know where you're going, you might just end up somewhere else."

The first stage of managing a project is determining the project goal. That tells you what you have to do, the conditions under which you have to do it, and (properly done) the priority relative to other projects and tasks in your schedule.

The first thing to remember about a project is that it is not an end in itself, but rather a means to an end. You do a project so that you can get the result. If you manage the wrong project—that is, if you get a different result—the project is a failure, even if you worked hard and followed good management procedures.

Sometimes it is challenging to pin down a project objective.

Every project begins with an underlying need. There is a problem that needs to be solved, or an opportunity that is available. You need to know not only what the project is, but also why you are doing it.

In Patrick's case, he needs to understand why the association is publishing this magazine. It could be any combination of the following, to:

- earn a profit for the association
- provide a public relations vehicle for member companies
- transmit industry information
- serve as a technical journal to help raise quality standards and solve complex problems.

These objectives are not mutually exclusive, of course. Likely, these reasons can be ranked in some sort of priority order. Is it more important to show a profit, or is it more important to provide quality technical information needed for industry engineers to develop new processes? Is it more important to provide public relations for member companies or to tabulate good industry information?

Understanding the reasons for the magazine will help set editorial policy, determine how to spend money, and affect the design and production standards, even the choice of paper stock.

From the basic reasons, you must define three elements of a good project, that is, the triple constraints:

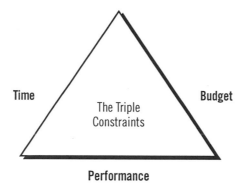

Time

The Triple
Constraints

Budget

Performance

Figure 4.1   The Triple Constraints: Time, Performance, and Budget

- how much time is available (called the *time constraint*)
- how much money or how many resources: people, tools, equipment you can use (called the *budget constraint*)
- what the end result must achieve (called the *performance criteria*).
  Put them all together, and you have the triple constraints (see Figure 4.1).
  You cannot manage a project successfully unless you know the triple constraints. They shape the world of the project.
  Take the case of Noah's ark. When God commanded Noah to build the ark, he set performance criteria:

> Make a boat from resinous wood, sealing it with tar, and construct decks and stalls throughout the ship. Make it 450 feet long, seventy-five feet wide, and forty-five feet high. Construct a skylight all the way around the ship, eighteen inches below the roof, and make three decks inside the boat—a bottom, middle, and upper deck—and put a door in the side.

All these performance criteria relate to the goal: to accommodate two of every animal and keep them safe from the flood. The deadline, of course, is that the ark had better be built before the flood. Budget? Not specified, but notice that the available resources are primarily the work effort of Noah and his sons.

One consequence of the triple constraints is that they are never ranked equally. The most important triple constraint is the *driver*. If you fail to achieve the driver, the project is always a failure. The next is the *middle constraint*. It is at least slightly less controlling than the driver; it may have more flexibility in its interpretation. The remaining one, the weak constraint, has the most flexibility.

In the case of Noah's ark, *budget* would have to be the weak constraint, since it is clearly most flexible. The question of whether time or performance is the driver would depend on whether God has fixed an absolute date when the flood will start (that would make time the driver), or whether God will hold off the flood until Noah finishes the ark (performance would become the driver).

Planning a Single Project

The choice of whether the driver is time or performance in this case would strongly affect how Noah approaches the work. If the deadline is absolute, and performance is slipping, perhaps he can trim some of the optional details, or finish up the stalls after the ark is floating. On the other hand, if performance is the driver, Noah can take some extra time, if needed, to make sure everything is shipshape. In both cases, the best solution would be to spend more money or more resources. Once the flood starts, leftover money will not be of much use.

The savvy project manager needs to know what the constraints are and understand their ranking. When things go well, these are not at issue. When things go wrong, you need to be able to use the flexibility of the weak and sometimes middle constraints to make sure you meet the driver, no matter what comes.

In the case of Patrick's magazine, assume that it is a general-interest magazine published first as a profit center for the association and second as a public-relations vehicle for the industry. The monthly deadline forms the time constraint, which is also the driver, since missing the deadline destroys the value of having a monthly magazine. The middle constraint is budget since the magazine needs to make a profit. While good public relations is important, it is also flexible in its definition. How many pages does each issue need? How much text is in each issue? These are subjective criteria and are therefore the most flexible. Performance criteria in this example are the weak constraint.

WORK BREAKDOWN STRUCTURE

The second step in managing a single project is creating the WBS, which is the equivalent of creating an *organization chart* for your project.

Step 1: Brainstorm tasks. List all the tasks that need to be completed to make your project a success.

Step 2: Group tasks into logical categories. You may use a variety of approaches to identify these categories, including departmental, skill, or phase. The goal of grouping the tasks is to improve management control.

Step 3: Display the tasks in an organizational chart. Figure 4.2 shows an example of the final product.

Tip! Use sticky notes to brainstorm the tasks. You will find it easier to group them together and create your WBS chart. Sticky notes are also valuable to the next step of managing your project.

NETWORK PLANNING

Now that you have a WBS, you know the tasks in your project, and you know which part of the project team is responsible for each task. Next, you have to put the tasks

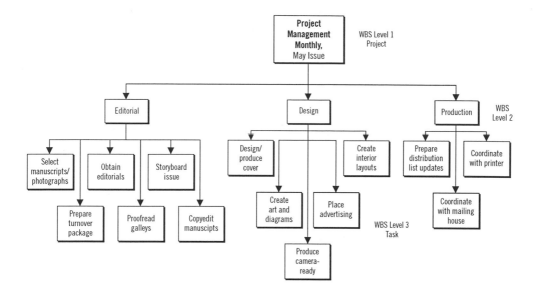

Figure 4.2   Work Breakdown Structure

into a project sequence. This stage is called *network planning*. You will hear the final result variously called a PERT chart or a CPM chart.

Program Evaluation and Review Technique and Critical Path Method

The program evaluation and review technique (PERT) and critical path method (CPM) are two powerful project management tools, both invented in the 1950s. PERT was developed by the United States Navy for managing the Polaris project; DuPont and Remington Rand developed CPM. While both were originally distinct approaches, they had strong similarities. In the real world of project management, people immediately began choosing those parts of each system they liked best, with the result that most people who use these systems today use a hybrid. For the purposes of everyday project management, PERT and CPM are effectively synonyms.

In this book, this kind of charting is called either PERT or network diagram.

Creating a Network Diagram

To create a *network diagram* (see Figure 4.3) or PERT chart of your project, take the sticky notes from the WBS and put them in the most logical and sensible order.

Tasks can be organized either in a d*ependent* or *parallel* manner. A dependent task is one that must wait for a predecessor task to complete. For example, in the diagram, Storyboard issue is dependent on Select manuscripts and photographs. You cannot start storyboarding (determining what goes on each page) until you know what the contents of the issue will be.

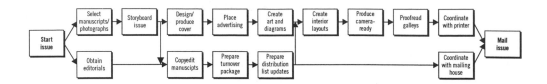

Figure 4.3   Network Diagram for Monthly Magazine

A parallel task is a task that can be performed in the same time frame as other tasks. For example, while you are selecting manuscripts and photographs and storyboarding the issue, you can Obtain editorials in parallel to those tasks. (This means pestering the president and executive director to turn over their manuscript copies. You already know that the editorials will be one page each in the magazine—that is a standard—so you can storyboard them even though you do not have the articles.)

The advantage of parallel tasking is that it saves time. Sometimes, parallel tasking increases resources needed, and sometimes it increases risk. You have to make strategic choices because there is more than one acceptable way to lay out a project.

Something very interesting happens when you make tasks parallel. Look at a close-up section of our network diagram in Figure 4.4.

Figure 4.4 shows an estimated time for each task, which is the next step you would follow in preparing your own network diagram. Notice that Start issue has a time of zero days; this is called a *milestone* in project management terms. Milestones identify major turning points in projects; they do not represent actual work to be done.

In this section of the project, you will see that all the tasks total sixteen days of work. Because of the parallel structure, this part of the project will take only twelve days to do—the longest path from start to copyedit. The *longest path* in a network diagram is very important; it is called the critical path, and a task on the critical path is called a *critical task.*

First, imagine what happens if either select manuscripts or storyboard goes over the time estimate. Immediately the bumper-car effect pushes out the start of copyedit. You just made the longest path longer, which makes the project longer.

Second, imagine what happens if the president is a day late with the editorial for this issue. That's right: nothing. Since the critical path segment between Start Issue and Copyedit manuscripts totals seven days (5 + 2), and Obtain editorials takes four days, Obtain editorials can be up to three days late (7 − 4) without impacting the start of the next task! Because Obtain editorials is not on the critical path, it is called a *non-critical task.*

Noncritical tasks are those that can be late without instantly bumping the start of the next critical task. The extra time available, called *slack* or *float*, is the difference between the critical path total and the noncritical path total.

Slack is your friend. Slack is an important tool in planning your project. Even if time is the driver, tasks with slack can be slipped in the schedule without harm to the

Figure 4.4   Critical Path Analysis for Monthly Magazine Tasks

ultimate deadline. In addition, if the slack task is done by a resource (person, equipment, tool), then *slack resource availability* may occur, which means that you have some resources not scheduled in that period. You can hold them back for emergencies, use them to get a head start on other work, or assign them to your other projects. (We will look at resource scheduling in much more detail later.)

Task Analysis

You can use forms to record and track the various pieces of information you need to manage your projects. A good *task analysis worksheet* (see Figure 4.5) lets you keep in a single place all the information you need to manage it. (It is a great help in delegating, too.)

While the form in Figure 4.5 is similar to the project control worksheet in Figure 2.1, the one depicted in Figure 4.5 is more detailed. The task analysis worksheet works better on larger projects with more complex tasks. Feel free to edit the format, based on issues and concerns specific to your own projects.

Tip! In managing multiple projects, you may find that many involve similar subject matter. When possible, reuse your task analysis forms to simplify planning and organization.

Here is a breakdown of each component of the task analysis form.

■ Task Number: Number your tasks (1, 2, 3, or A, B, C)—a common shortcut. If you use a project management software package, your program will automatically number your tasks.

■ Task Name: Give each task a distinct name.

■ Predecessor/Successor Task(s): From your network diagram, write down the tasks immediately prior to the current task (predecessors) and the tasks immediately following the current task (successors).

■ Specifications/Deliverables: Define what the task must accomplish to be considered complete.

Task No:	Task Name:

Predecessor Task(s):	Successor Task(s):

Specifications/Deliverables:

- _____
- _____
- _____

Resources—People/Department

- _____
- _____
- _____

Equipment/Supplies

- _____
- _____
- _____

Time Estimate

"Must Start" _____   "Must Finish" _____

Milestones

- _____
- _____
- _____

Optimistic _____   Pessimistic _____   Most Likely _____

Cost Estimate

Salaries	$ _____
Equipment/Supplies	$ _____
Contract Costs	$ _____
Overhead @ _____ %	$ _____
TOTAL	$ _____

Figure 4.5   Sample Format for a Task Analysis Worksheet

- Resources: Include people as well as tools/equipment.
- Time Estimate: For a simple project, fill in only the *most likely* item in this block. More complex projects may require more detailed estimating. For example, normal tasks are assumed to begin when their predecessors are complete. If the predecessor finishes early, the task starts early; if the predecessor is late, it starts late. However, some tasks have calendar date issues. Our magazine must be at the printer on a certain date, so the final galley proofs must be ready then—no matter what!

Milestones show the completion of parts of the task. In *design/produce cover*, one milestone might be *cover photo selected*, followed by *pencil rough of cover completed*, and finally *cover master artwork produced*. Use milestones for finer control of what is going on in the middle of a task.

- Cost Estimate: Figure costs by category. Every organization has its own internal financial procedures. Your project may or may not be charged certain costs, from staff salaries to equipment and supplies, including percentages for overhead and general administrative expenses.

Tip! Filling out forms requires a lot of work. Here are two shortcuts. First, you may delegate completing the form to team members and subordinate project managers. Second, you may be able to reuse (with some editing) forms you have already designed.

Estimating Techniques

How long will each task take? On some projects, it is easy to predict how long a task will take. If you are going to send somebody to a three-day training course, you expect it is going to take three days, not two and not four. On the other hand, if the task is to create a new idea, it is hard to predict accurately how long it will take. Try some of these techniques to improve your estimating skills.

Six Steps to Exceptional Estimating

1. Use actual time estimates from similar tasks in other projects. Good estimates are based on historical data; use the best historical data you can find.

2. Involve the people most knowledgeable, and ask for their estimates. Be sure to learn their tendencies. Are they optimists or pessimists? (Some people claim to be realists. They are usually pessimists.)

3. Research the history of vendors and subcontractors you plan to use. How experienced are they? How good have their estimates been in the past? Get references, and check them out.

4. Consult standard reference books containing time estimates. From the standard garage manual that estimates the time a mechanic should take to fix your car to software industry norms for the development of code, many references exist for specific work. Check your trade or professional organization for details.

5. Watch for tasks with outcome and timing that directly affect the project final outcome. When possible, build in extra time and resources to allow slack for those tasks.

6. Train yourself to be an exceptional estimator. Whenever you need an estimate, make a guess and write it down. Then make an estimate. When you finish the actual work, compare the result to your guess. By giving your brain regular feedback, you will find yourself getting progressively accurate.

PERT Time Estimating

One of the more challenging parts of estimating involves uncertainty. How long a job will take can depend on unpredictable factors. For example, if a construction company cannot build in the rain, the number of rainy days in the construction season affects how long the job will take.

The creators of the PERT project management system used a statistical approach to uncertainty. For each task, they created three estimates:
- the optimistic (best case) situation, called $T(o)$
- the pessimistic (worst case) situation, called $T(p)$
- the most likely situation, called $T(m)$.

Even though it is impossible to predict what a given task will take, if you have a large enough project, you can reasonably expect some good luck, some bad luck, and a great deal of average luck. Therefore, you can create a weighted average (called $T(e)$, short for time estimate) of the three times by using the formula:

$$T(e) = T(o) + (4 \star T(m)) + T(p)$$

Note: For an explanation of the full statistical process, consult *Practical Project Management* by Michael Dobson.

If you calculate $T(e)$ for all tasks in your project, and use those tasks in making up your schedule, you will find that although individual tasks may run over or under the estimated time, your actual schedule should come out nearly on time.

How close? There is a statistical answer to that, and it has to do with a concept called *standard deviation*, abbreviated with the Greek letter σ or *sigma*. You determine the sigma of a task with the following formula:

$$\sigma = \frac{T(p) - T(o)}{6}$$

According to standard probability theory:
- 68.26 percent of the time the work will be completed $\pm$ 1 s of $T(e)$
- 95.44% of the time the work will be completed $\pm$ 2 s of $T(e)$
- 99.73% of the time the work will be completed $\pm$ 3 s of $T(e)$.

That is the process for one task. There is one catch. If you are trying to calculate sigma for a sequence of tasks, take each task sigma, square it, add the squares together, and then take the square root of the sum.

You use the standard deviation concept in project management to determine the risk level and additional time you require. The ideal project has a safety margin of two sigmas of the critical (longest) path, because it then has a 95 percent probability of being finished on time, even if things go wrong. If you cannot add that much safety margin (and often you cannot), you can at least add as much as is available. With a

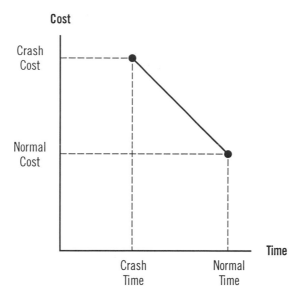

Figure 4.6   Graph Depicting Crash Slope

standard statistical table, you can figure the percentage chance you have of finishing the project on time. This is called the *confidence level*.

Not all project managers use this technique. Utilize it only if your projects have high uncertainty factors and you need extra time to meet your deadline. It is simpler to use than it may appear. Once you put the formulas into a spreadsheet program, the process of calculating becomes quite speedy.

Critical Path Method Time Estimating

Another approach to time estimating evolves from the idea that, quite often, if one person can do the job in three weeks, two people may be able to do the job faster.

Speeding up a task by giving it extra resources—people, tools, equipment, or money—is called *crashing* the task. Not all tasks can be crashed. If you are trying to get the editorial copy from the president, two people will likely not have any better luck than one person.

The process of crash analysis is figuring your crash options and determining whether or not they are worthwhile (see Figure 4.6).

Imagine the following situation:

- One person can do the job in three weeks at a salary of $1,000 per week.
       Normal Time = 3 weeks   Normal Cost = $3,000

- Two people can do the job in two weeks at a salary of $1,000 per week each.
       Crash Time = 2 weeks   Crash Cost = $4,000

The *crash slope* is the difference between the normal and crash situations.

$$\text{Crash Slope} = (-1 \text{ week}, +\$1,000)$$

In other words, you save a week and spend an extra $1,000. Now the question becomes: "Is it worth it?"

To determine whether a task is worth crashing, first see if the task is on the critical path. If it is not on the critical path, saving time on the task will not save time on the project. It will just create more slack. (On the other hand, if the noncritical task is very risky, you might put the extra resources there to make the project safer.)

If the task is on the critical path, now you have to determine the value to the project being a week early. Is finishing early worth $1,000? Consider not only the value of turning over the project results but also the fact that you will no longer be spending money, people, and resources in the week you saved.

Sometimes it is clear that crashing is worthwhile; if this is the case, do it. Sometimes it is clear that crashing is a very bad idea; if this is the case, do not do it. Sometimes the situation is difficult to call. If so, try postponing the decision until later in your project. You might discover that changing situations in the project may tip the crash decision one way or another. If you are running late and racking up overtime, the value of crashing may be positive. But if everything is going great, the cost of crashing may not be worthwhile.

The only other tip on crash time is to remember that if you promise your boss you will save a week by spending the $1,000, save the week!

Task Table

The final element you need to put together a project schedule is called a *task table* (see Figure 4.7). Fortunately, everything you need to put a table together follows the previous process. You simply organize a table that contains:

■ a list of tasks (from your sticky-note PERT chart)

■ an estimate of the time each task will take to complete (regular or PERT estimates, whichever you have decided to use)

■ a list of predecessor tasks (also from your sticky-note PERT chart).

You may number your tasks and use these numbers to list your predecessors and speed up the process.

You have already made estimates for a few of the tasks in publishing the magazine issue. Now it is time to fill in the rest and build the task table.

GANTT CHARTING

The final stage of developing your project plan is to make a Gantt chart. You will draw the chart in this chapter, then learn how to use it effectively in Chapter 5.

The Gantt chart is one of the most important tools of effective project management. It was developed by Henry L. Gantt, an ordnance engineer at Aberdeen Proving Grounds in Maryland during World War I. Gantt charts are relatively easy to prepare and enormously useful.

Task No.	Task Name	Time Estimate	Predecessors
1	Start issue	0 days	None
2	Select manuscript and photographs	5 days	1
3	Obtain editorials	4 days	1
4	Storyboard issue	2 days	2
5	Copyedit manuscripts	5 days	3, 4
6	Design/produce cover	2 days	4
7	Place advertising	2 days	6
8	Prepare turnover package	1 day	5
9	Create art and diagrams	4 days	7, 8
10	Prepare distribution list updates	1 day	8
11	Create interior layout	2 days	9
12	Produce camera-ready art	2 days	11
13	Proofread galleys	2 days	12
14	Coordinate with printer	6 days	13
15	Coordinate with mailing house	2 days	10
16	Mail issue	0 days	14, 15

Figure 4.7   Project Task Table

A Gantt chart in its simplest form is a timeline that shows the tasks in your project in terms of the calendar time they occupy. You may prepare them by hand or you may use one of a number of computer software programs that prepares them automatically. These programs may do PERT charts and perform other technical aspects of project management for you. Software options will be discussed in Chapter 5. Before you consider buying project management software, be sure you can do charting for simple projects by hand; this will help you learn what the software is trying to accomplish.

You can create a Gantt chart with a sheet of graph paper, or you may use the *Gantt chart grid* in Figure 4.8.

Task No.	Task Name	1	2	3	4	5	6	7	8	9	10	11	12	13	14	15	16	17

Figure 4.8   A Sample Gantt Chart Grid

Create Your Own Gantt Chart

You will need graph paper and a straight edge for drawing.

You have a project and a task table. Your assignment is to draw a timeline and determine the critical path for the project.

PROJECT: Buy a Project Management Software Package

The accompanying Gantt chart grid provides the task numbers and task names for this exercise.

Task No.	Task Name	Time Estimate	Predecessors
1	Needs analysis	5 days	N/A
2	Choose computer	4 days	1
3	Choose software	3 days	1
4	Purchase	1 day	2, 3
5	Delivery time	5 days	4
6	Train user	3 days	4
7	Install system	1 day	5
8	Acceptance	1 day	6, 7

Start with the first task, Needs analysis. Since the task has no dependencies, it starts at the beginning of the project. Draw a line from the beginning of the first day to the end of the fifth day because the task takes five days.

Task No.	Task Name	1	2	3	4	5	6	7	8	9	10	11	12	13	14	15	16	17
1	Needs analysis																	
2	Choose computer																	
3	Choose software																	
4	Purchase																	
5	Delivery time																	
6	Train user																	
7	Install system																	
8	Acceptance																	

Task No.	Task Name	1	2	3	4	5	6	7	8	9	10	11	12	13	14	15	16	17
1	Needs analysis	███	███	███	███	███												
2	Choose computer																	
3	Choose software																	
4	Purchase																	
5	Delivery time																	
6	Train user																	
7	Install system																	
8	Acceptance																	

So far, so good. The next two tasks are both dependent on Task 1. If two tasks are dependent on the same predecessor, they are parallel to each other. That means that the Gantt chart bars for tasks 2 and 3 should start after the end of the Gantt chart bar for Task 1.

Now, draw tasks 2 and 3 on your Gantt chart.

Task No.	Task Name	1	2	3	4	5	6	7	8	9	10	11	12	13	14	15	16	17
1	Needs analysis	███	███	███	███	███												
2	Choose computer																	
3	Choose software																	
4	Purchase																	
5	Delivery time																	
6	Train user																	
7	Install system																	
8	Acceptance																	

Task 4 has two predecessors; it is dependent on both tasks 2 and 3. Therefore, it cannot start until both predecessors are complete; Task 4 starts after all its predecessors. Now, draw Task 4 on your Gantt chart.

Task No.	Task Name	1	2	3	4	5	6	7	8	9	10	11	12	13	14	15	16	17
1	Needs analysis	■	■	■	■	■												
2	Choose computer						■	■	■	■								
3	Choose software						■	■	■									
4	Purchase										■							
5	Delivery time																	
6	Train user																	
7	Install system																	
8	Acceptance																	

You have worked through the various types of Gantt-chart relationships. Now, finish your Gantt chart to see how long the project will take.

Task No.	Task Name	1	2	3	4	5	6	7	8	9	10	11	12	13	14	15	16	17
1	Needs analysis	■	■	■	■	■												
2	Choose computer						■	■	■	■								
3	Choose software						■	■	■									
4	Purchase										■							
5	Delivery time											■	■	■	■	■		
6	Train user											■	■	■				
7	Install system																■	
8	Acceptance																	■

Looking at the timeline, you now know that this project should take seventeen days to complete. This is the first useful thing a Gantt chart can tell you.

The next step is to determine which are the *critical* and which are the *noncritical* tasks.

Earlier in this chapter, you learned the concept of the critical path. A task is critical if delaying it instantly delays the project; it is noncritical if it has slack, or extra time, before it bumps the start of the next critical task.

Note on your finished Gantt chart the tasks that are critical and noncritical. On noncritical tasks, note how much slack is available.

Task No.	Task Name	1	2	3	4	5	6	7	8	9	10	11	12	13	14	15	16	17
1	Needs analysis	███	███	███	███	███												
2	Choose computer						███	███	███	███								
3	Choose software						▒▒▒	▒▒▒	▒▒▒	▒▒▒								
4	Purchase										███							
5	Delivery time											███	███	███	███	███		
6	Train user											▒▒▒	▒▒▒	░░░	░░░	░░░		
7	Install system																███	
8	Acceptance																	███

███ Critical   ▒▒▒ Noncritical   ░░░ Available slack

There are two noncritical tasks in this project: Task 3, Choose software, and Task 6, Train user.

Task 3 has one day of slack, since Task 4, Purchase, is waiting for Task 2, Choose computer, to finish.

Task 6, Train user, has three days of slack—not two! Notice that according to the task table, Task 7, Install system, is only dependent on Task 5, Delivery time. If Task 6 is late, Task 7 can still go ahead. Task 8, Acceptance, is the only task waiting for Train user to finish. Task 6 can therefore be up to three days late without jeopardizing the start of a critical task.

Congratulations! You have successfully completed a Gantt chart. In Chapter 5, you will learn how to use it.

How to Read and Use a Gantt Chart

"I've seen lots of timeline charts," Patrick observed. "In fact, you have a magnetic scheduling board hanging on the wall. Yes, it shows the sequence and the deadline, but it seems like an awful lot of work."

Patrick's information needs about his projects not only involve time but also issues such as the following.

- *How many people do I need to accomplish the work?*
- *How do I assign and schedule people to get the most accomplished?*
- *How can I reorganize my project if my deadlines get cut?*
- *How do I track and monitor the actual performance of the work compared to the original plan?*

The Gantt chart, properly used and understood, can help Patrick with a number of these problems.

DEFINITIONS

Here are the key terms you will need to understand for this chapter.

A *Gantt chart* is a timeline chart that shows the sequence of tasks in a project over a calendar period.

Project management software is one of various software packages that create and calculate project management charts, such as Gantt, PERT, and CPM.

A *resource* includes people, tools, equipment, and money that one must assign and allocate to get the work done.

Resource planning is the process of determining how to get the best use of people, equipment, tools, and money to get the job done.

A *lag activity* is a task that requires you to allocate time but no resources.

A *slack resource* is a resource without a job during some periods of a project.

Resource overload occurs when more jobs than resources exist during some periods of a project.

Leveling is rearranging a schedule to eliminate resource overloads.

Leveling within slack is rearranging a schedule without letting the deadline slip.

A *resource Gantt chart* is a Gantt chart that shows how resources are allocated.

A *tracking Gantt chart* is a Gantt chart that allows comparison of the actual to the plan for project tasks.

GANTT CHARTING FOR SINGLE PROJECTS

The *Gantt chart* in Figure 5.1 uses the task table from Chapter 4 (see Figure 4.7) and applies the Gantt chart techniques in the last exercise.

This chart aided the creation of a computer program called Microsoft Project. To make the chart, task-table data is entered in the project window, and the program does the rest, including determining the critical path.

Computer Software in Project Management

If you do not have a problem, do not try to fix it with a computer. This is always good advice but particularly in the area of project management software, which once won a category award in a computer magazine for "type of software most often purchased merely to sit unopened on the shelf."

In the same way that a word processing system is of little use to someone who does not know how to type, project management software is absolutely no use to someone who does not know how to create Gantt charts and other tools by hand. If you already know how to use the tools, a computer can speed up the work, do the arithmetic, keep good records, and draw diagrams neatly. Although these are considerable benefits, they do not constitute *project management*. Project management is what project managers do, not what software does. It would be more accurate to say that there is no such thing as project management software—rather, there is project tracking and scheduling software.

Project management software will do some or all of the following: create Gantt, PERT, and CPM charts from task-table information (you still have to do the task table yourself); allow assignment of resources to tasks; keep track of your resource scheduling; signal conflicts between resource availability and workload; track resources allocated among projects; create task lists; compare plan to actual task accomplishment; calculate the critical path; and more. Updating ease and the ability to look at multiple options are other advantages.

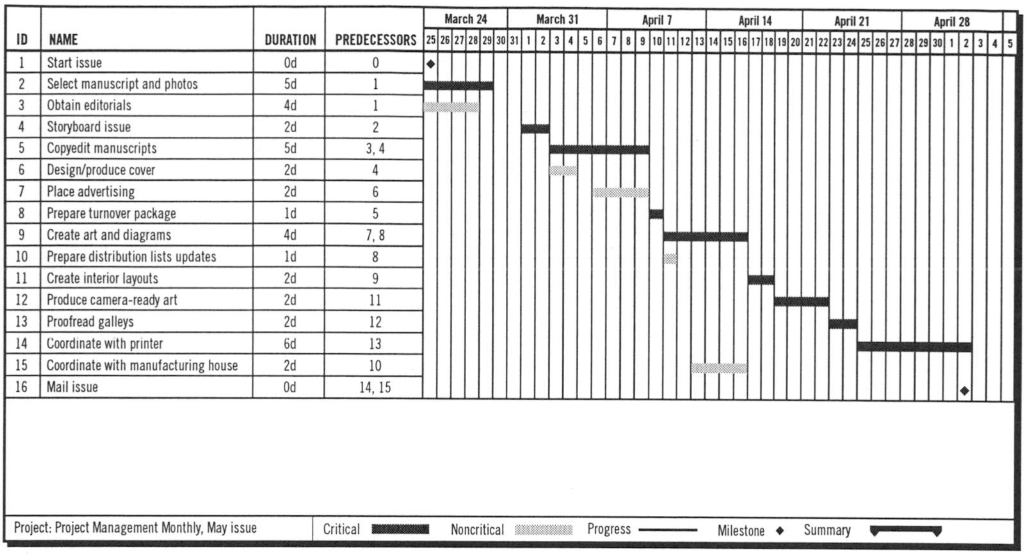

ID	NAME	DURATION	PREDECESSORS	March 24	March 31	April 7	April 14	April 21	April 28
1	Start issue	0d	0						
2	Select manuscript and photos	5d	1						
3	Obtain editorials	4d	1						
4	Storyboard issue	2d	2						
5	Copyedit manuscripts	5d	3, 4						
6	Design/produce cover	2d	4						
7	Place advertising	2d	6						
8	Prepare turnover package	1d	5						
9	Create art and diagrams	4d	7, 8						
10	Prepare distribution lists updates	1d	8						
11	Create interior layouts	2d	9						
12	Produce camera-ready art	2d	11						
13	Proofread galleys	2d	12						
14	Coordinate with printer	6d	13						
15	Coordinate with manufacturing house	2d	10						
16	Mail issue	0d	14, 15						

Project: Project Management Monthly, May issue | Critical ▮▮▮ | Noncritical ▨▨▨ | Progress ——— | Milestone ◆ | Summary ▼———▼

Figure 5.1   Gantt Chart for Monthly Magazine Issue

The availability and ease of use of project management software have improved remarkably in the last several years. Many project managers who previously found software too complicated now find it useful. Much good software is now available, and the field is changing rapidly. Read test reports in leading computer magazines, analyze your needs, and shop accordingly. Do not focus attention on price of the package; the least expensive part of using software will be the cost of the software itself. Most of the real cost will be user time.

Project management software packages fall into a few categories. These are power categories, not quality categories.

Major projects. For the very largest projects ($10 million plus), purchase comprehensive packages that run on mainframes and networks. Primavera is one well-known package in this category.

Medium projects. The most popular category of project management software includes titles such as Workbench, Timeline, SuperProject, and Microsoft Project. This category of full-featured programs allows management of projects containing up to one thousand or fifteen hundred tasks comfortably. Most cost from $400 to $700.

Small projects. For basic Gantt charting, small projects, or other projects not using resource planning software, numerous packages including FastTrack Scheduler, InstaPlan 5000, and OnTarget are available. Some organizer software packages and personal information managers now include Gantt-chart functions. Some shareware (EasyProject) works at this level.

Nonproject management software. "If the only tool you have is a hammer, all problems look like nails." Use the right tools for the job. In addition to formal project management software, you can use spreadsheets, drawing programs, flowcharters, and other tools.

INTERPRETING YOUR GANTT CHART

For a tool that is so visually simple and clear, the Gantt chart is surprisingly rich and powerful in helping you understand your project and solving problems.

Five Ways to Use a Gantt Chart for Project Management Success

Use Gantt charts to:

1. See how long the project will take.
2. Prepare easy-to-read and easy-to-understand reports for management, customers, and team members.
3. Determine resource requirements for your project.
4. Determine who must do each job.
5. Measure your progress.

The following discussion examines how to use a Gantt chart to achieve project management success.

See How Long the Project Will Take

When you drew your own Gantt chart in the exercise that ended Chapter 4 and reviewed the computer-drawn Gantt chart that began this chapter, the first piece of information you obtained is how long the project will take. The hand-drawn Gantt chart shows working days: exactly seventeen. There are twenty-three days of scheduled activities, but the project ends up taking seventeen days because some tasks are parallel (see Figure 5.2).

The more sophisticated computer-drawn chart includes an allowance for weekends. If a task takes five days and starts on Thursday, it ends the following Wednesday. The computer will also allow you to mark holidays and vacations for individual staff members on the internal calendar, and it will adjust your tasks accordingly.

If your plan shows that you will finish on or ahead of schedule, then you are ready for the next step. But what if it does not?

Imagine that your boss tells you that you have fifteen days available to buy the project management software. Your plan says it will take you seventeen days. Have you made a mistake in your Gantt chart?

No, you have not. In a more complex project with many parallel activities, sometimes there is no easy way to tell how you are doing until you finish the task table and draw your first Gantt chart. Neither is it unusual nor is it a sign of poor planning to find that your first-draft Gantt chart shows you to be over schedule; however, you cannot stop with your first draft.

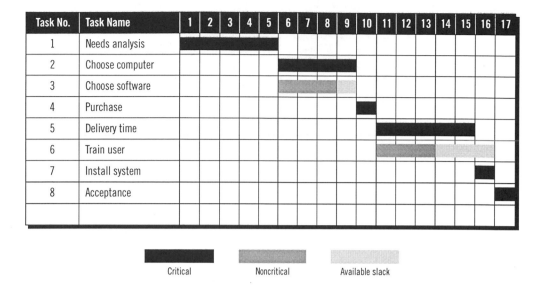

Task No.	Task Name	1	2	3	4	5	6	7	8	9	10	11	12	13	14	15	16	17
1	Needs analysis	███	███	███	███	███												
2	Choose computer						███	███	███	███								
3	Choose software						▒▒▒	▒▒▒	▒▒▒	▒▒▒								
4	Purchase										███							
5	Delivery time											███	███	███	███	███		
6	Train user											▒▒▒	▒▒▒	▒▒▒	░░░	░░░		
7	Install system																███	
8	Acceptance																	███

Critical   Noncritical   Available slack

Figure 5.2   Gantt Chart Showing Shortened Schedule Accomplished with Parallel Tasking

What can you do? When your plan shows you to be over schedule, and you need to shorten the plan, try one of these ideas: crash tasks, make more tasks parallel, or reduce scope.

Crash tasks. Remember, *crashing* a task means that you add resources in order to lower time. You might, for example, put two people onto Needs analysis if you feel that would cut the time needed by two days. Putting two people on Choose software to save two days would not work because that task is noncritical. Shortening a non-critical task will not speed up the project; it will give you more slack.

Extra resources are not only extra people. Take a look at Task 5 in Figure 5.2, Delivery time. Imagine that you are ordering our computer and software from a mail order house. This is called a lag activity, a task that involves time (waiting for the box to arrive) but no work (you can do other things while waiting for the box). What if you paid for express delivery?

Say there are two options in the mail order catalog besides regular delivery: overnight, which would reduce the task to one day, and second day, which would reduce the task to two days. Which is the better choice if time is of the essence?

Common sense says that overnight delivery is faster than second-day delivery but not in this case (see Figure 5.3). If you make Delivery time a one-day task, it takes one more day to Install system. That is two days; but Train user takes three days! Whether Delivery time takes one or two days, Task 8, Acceptance, starts at the same time. In project management language, *it is usually not productive to crash a task more than the slack available on the noncritical parallel path.*

How to Read and Use a Gantt Chart

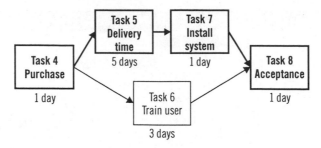

Original Plan: Critical Path is 1+5+1+1=8 days.

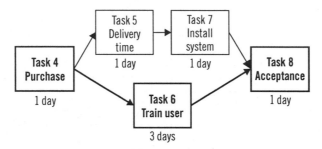

Overnigh Delivery: Critical Path is now 1+3+1=5 days.

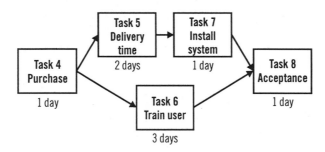

Second-Day: Both paths are critical (1+2+1+1=1+3+1, or 5 days either way).

Figure 5.3   Critical Path Can Be Shortened by Crashing Critical Tasks

The exception is that sometimes you can crash a task to lower risk elsewhere in the project. If you believe that Install system is particularly risky, you might choose overnight delivery because you wanted a day's margin in the project.

Make more tasks parallel. You may go back to your original sticky-note PERT chart and ask yourself if more tasks can be made parallel. Say that you want to use express delivery. Remember, these strategies for shortening your project can be combined. You could, in theory, start the training as soon as you decide which software package you are going to buy, as long as you do it out-of-house.

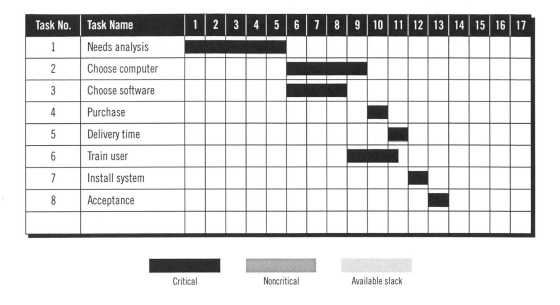

Task No.	Task Name	1	2	3	4	5	6	7	8	9	10	11	12	13	14	15	16	17
1	Needs analysis	██	██	██	██	██												
2	Choose computer						██	██	██	██								
3	Choose software						██	██										
4	Purchase										██							
5	Delivery time											██						
6	Train user									██	██	██						
7	Install system												██					
8	Acceptance													██				

██ Critical   ▓▓ Noncritical   ░░ Available slack

Figure 5.4   Gantt Chart Showing Additional Options for Shortening Critical Path

If you make Train user dependent on Choose software, notice you now can go with overnight delivery to save more time!

Now the critical path is only thirteen days—but all tasks are now critical. The lack of any slack indicates that the risk of this project has increased somewhat, but you still have two days to hit your fifteen-day target.

Remember, any project can normally be laid out in different ways. Make sure you know the various options beforehand, so you can make the choice that is strategically best for your project.

Reduce scope. Similar to crashing, reducing scope means deciding to do less work on a given task, which will reduce time. One example is to do a less-detailed needs analysis rather than a comprehensive one. That allows completion of the project in two or three days. Or you might decide that you are only going to look in a certain range of computers and ignore everything else. That would cut Task 2 back a day. Reducing scope is not necessarily reducing quality. You have to focus on what is important and what is not. Sometimes a project experiences mission creep, when many optional (and possibly unimportant) work assignments add up to a serious burden.

If you are cutting trivia, then you can reduce the scope of certain tasks without harming project quality.

Prepare Easy-to-Read and Easy-to-Understand Reports for Management, Customers, and Team Members

Even if your project has complex needs, many of your managers, customers, and team members will need less-detailed information. The clarity and simplicity of a Gantt

Task No.	Task Name	1	2	3	4	5	6	7	8	9	10
1	Plan logistics	■	■	□							
2	Plan events	■	■	■							
3	Select site				■						
4	Develop publicity				■	■	■				
5	Conduct publicity								■	▨	□
6	Design booths				■	■					
7	Develop site plan					■					
8	Pre-event logistics						■	■	■		
9	Set up event									■	■

■ Critical   ▨ Noncritical   □ Available slack

Figure 5.5 Gantt Chart Grid Showing a Special Event Plan

chart makes it an ideal tool for management-reporting requirements. It is visual, has a high impact, and does not require special training in project management to interpret. Project management software programs often allow you to print your project schedule with varying detail and specificity. Select more simple charts for people with more general information needs.

Determine Resource Requirements for Your Project

One of the greatest challenges in managing single or multiple projects is figuring team size and assigning and allocating people and other resources to project tasks. A Gantt chart can be an extremely helpful tool in resource planning.

Now look at a slightly more complex project to illustrate the various ways you can allocate resources on your project (see Figure 5.5).

In the project in Figure 5.5, you are planning a special event. You have the basic Gantt chart and now must plan resource needs. Assuming each bar on the Gantt chart represents one person working full time for each period, and assuming that all people on the team have all the skills necessary to do the tasks, what is the optimum size of the project team for this project? Follow these steps.

1. Determine resources needed in each period. Add the number of bars in each column. You will see the answer in Figure 5.6.

If your situation is more complex (some jobs require less than one full-time person; others require more than one person), you will need to note on each bar how many person-hours of work are required, then add those numbers.

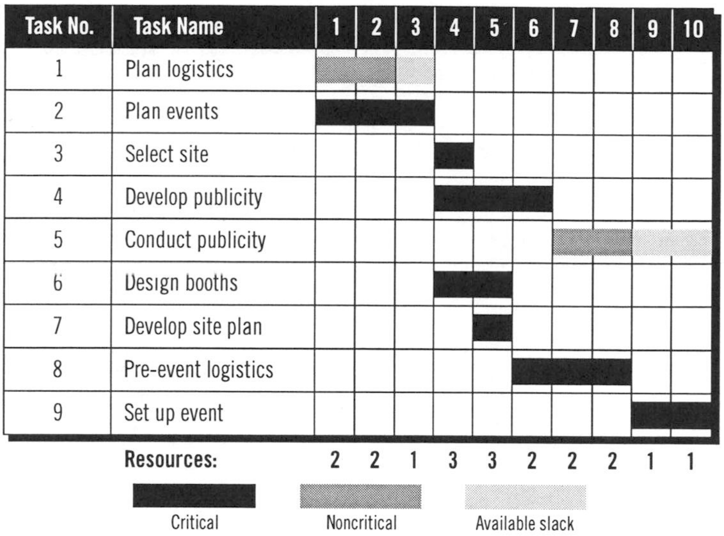

Task No.	Task Name	1	2	3	4	5	6	7	8	9	10
1	Plan logistics	▨	▨								
2	Plan events	█	█	█							
3	Select site				█						
4	Develop publicity				█	█					
5	Conduct publicity							▨	▨	░	░
6	Design booths				█	█					
7	Develop site plan					█					
8	Pre-event logistics						█	█	█		
9	Set up event									█	█
Resources:		2	2	1	3	3	2	2	2	1	1

█ Critical ▨ Noncritical ░ Available slack

Figure 5.6 Gantt Chart Grid Showing the Resources Needed for a Certain Period for a Special Event Plan

2. Determine greatest, smallest, and median resource requirements. The greatest resource requirement in any given period is three. The smallest resource requirement is one. In the majority of weeks, however, you need two.

3. Use the median resource requirement as your standard. Your project team should consist of two people.

4. Determine what to do with underutilized resources. You have two potential problems. In three days (Day 3, Day 9, and Day 10) of your project, you are paying two people, but you have work for one. The person without a job those days is called a slack resource. Is that a bad thing? Not necessarily.

First, you do not assume everything in the project will go perfectly, because that is frequently not the case. A little slack resource time lowers project risk. Use the resource if things go wrong. If nothing goes wrong, find something else for that resource to do (such as help somebody else to speed up his task).

Second, slack resources can be used for crashing other tasks. If you find slack resource time in your project, for which you have to pay, look for crash opportunities. They may be a bargain.

Third, since you are dealing with multiple projects, a slack resource can be moved to work on other projects during any slack periods. (You will learn how to do that in much greater detail later.)

5. Figure what to do when you have more work than resources. You have a much tougher problem during days 4 and 5 of your schedule, when you have jobs for three people and two people on your team. Deal with periods of resource overload in one of two ways.

Task No.	Task Name	1	2	3	4	5	6	7	8	9	10
1	Plan logistics	▓	▓	░							
2	Plan events	■	■	■							
3	Select site				■						
4	Develop publicity					■	■				
5	Conduct publicity									■	■
6	Design booths							■	■		
7	Develop site plan					■					
8	Pre-event logistics						■	■	■		
9	Set up event									■	■
Resources:		2	2	1	2	2	2	2	2	2	2

■ Critical   ▓ Noncritical   ░ Available slack

Figure 5.7 Gantt Chart Grid Showing Leveling within Slack

■ Get more resources. Not all project resources have to be on the project from start to finish. Temporary resources, including overtime work, borrowing someone from elsewhere in the organization, hiring temporary workers, or contracting out may be available. If you can get someone outside our regular team to come in and do Task 6, Design booths, then you will be able to complete the rest of the work according to schedule.

■ Level the schedule. Rearrange the project schedule to avoid resource overload. This is called leveling the project. When you make any two tasks parallel, assume that you have (or can get) resources to do the jobs at the same time. If that is not true, then you cannot make the jobs parallel after all. When time is not the project driver, leveling is not necessarily bad news. The project just takes a little longer.

When time is the driver, you can only *level within slack*. This means that you look for ways to shift noncritical tasks so that they do not bump any critical tasks and still eliminate any resource overloads. This is not always possible but is often worth trying. When successful, it makes the resource problem go away without pushing out the deadline.

In the sample project, slack time is available in days 9 and 10. The booths do not need to be ready until the start of Task 9, Set up event. You can move Task 6 into days 7 and 8, but that shifts the resource overload; it does not make it go away. Task 5, Conduct publicity, has two days of slack. If you move Task 5 so that it is parallel with Task 9, all of the overload goes away. You have successfully leveled within slack.

Remember, nothing is perfect. Although you have eliminated the resource overload and kept the project on schedule without spending money on additional resources, you have also eliminated most of the slack and made another task critical. This increases project risk. As a project manager of single or multiple projects, you frequently make risk/time/budget tradeoffs in deciding how best to achieve your goals.

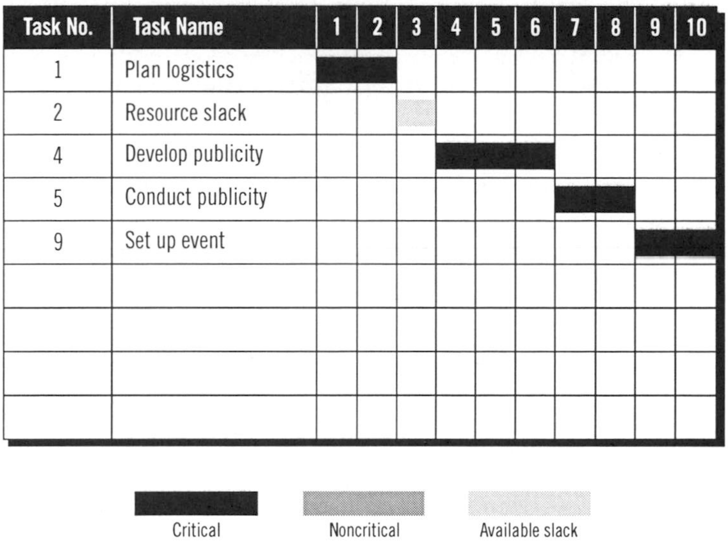

Task No.	Task Name	1	2	3	4	5	6	7	8	9	10
1	Plan logistics	█	█								
2	Resource slack			░							
4	Develop publicity				█	█	█				
5	Conduct publicity							█	█		
9	Set up event									█	█

█ Critical   ▓ Noncritical   ░ Available slack

Figure 5.8 Resource Gantt Chart Showing How a Team Member's Time Will Be Used on a Project

Determine Who Must Do Each Job

Determining team size is important. The next step is to assign our team. Consider nonleveled project, and have a team of two full-timers and one temporary person.

You know that the temporary person will do Task 6, Design booths; that leaves two people to do all remaining tasks: Sam and Gary. Assign Sam to Task 1, Plan logistics, and put Gary on Task 2, Plan events.

Sam will finish at the end of Day 2. To find his next job assignment, look down the next column in Figure 5.8 and see that no task starts on Day 3. Sam is a slack resource for that day. You may keep him in reserve for problems, have him help Gary on Task 2, or assign him to other work within the department.

Gary finishes Task 2 at the end of Day 3. Now, Gary and Sam are both available for new tasks. Looking down the Day 4 column, we see that three tasks start. One of them, Task 6, is already assigned. It is at this point that you must do skill matching for jobs.

The first possibility is that Sam has the skills to do either of the jobs. In that case, wait and schedule other team members who may be more limited in expertise, then have Sam do what remains.

The second possibility is that Sam has the technical skill to do one job but not the other. In that case, Sam has to be assigned the job for which he has skills, and Gary takes the other one.

The third possibility is that Sam does not have the technical skills to do either of the jobs starting on Day 4. Now what? Sam would then become another slack resource, and you would have a resource overload in Day 4. You either find something for Sam to do elsewhere, get another temporary resource, or level the schedule to cope with the resource overload. (This does not mean that Sam is not a valuable employee. It means that the skills needed that day do not match what your team has to offer. Now, if Sam cannot do *any* of the jobs in the project, he is on the wrong team. This is much less common.)

You continue through the project, assigning Sam and Gary to tasks. If you are using project management software, it will often allow you to assign people to tasks and will keep track of how much they have been delegated. In more complex projects, the theory is no more involved than that described, but the arithmetic can become beastly.

Especially in managing multiple projects, but also in managing a single large project, it is important to keep track of assignments. You can use a Gantt chart to help. Since it shows how work is allocated over time, you can draw a *resource Gantt chart* (see Figure 5.8) showing how a resource can be used just as easily as a project is managed. If you are using project management software, your program may create a resource Gantt chart automatically.

Notice that in Sam's case, there cannot be any parallel bars (that would mean he is working sixteen hours that day). If the jobs take partial rather than full days, Sam's schedule can include overlaps.

Resource Gantt charts have a number of uses. First, they help a project manager keep track of staff assignments. Second, they help team members track their own schedules and identify potential conflicts well in advance of trouble.

Third, and possibly most important, when managing multiple projects using the same staff, you can find cross-project dependencies, where someone's delay on one task in Project A can affect another task in Project B—because the same person is scheduled to do both tasks. The resource Gantt chart, listing all tasks in all projects for each team member, helps identify those problems and allows solving them in advance.

Measure Your Progress

The final way you can use a Gantt chart is to measure progress. This is called a *Tracking Gantt Chart* (see Figure 5.9), and it facilitates seeing the consequences of various project events.

Refer to the Gantt chart you completed at the end of Chapter 4.

You will notice that the bars have changed pattern and size (see Figure 5.10); they now represent the original plan. To make a tracking Gantt chart, you keep the original plan, then draw in new bars to accurately represent how long the tasks take, not how long you think they will take.

What happened on the project?

The first thing you will notice is that Task 1 took one day less than scheduled. That means tasks 2 and 3, both dependent on Task 1, could start a day early. Unfortunately, Task 3 went a day over schedule.

Does that make things even? You gained a day and lost a day, but you are still a day ahead. The day you gained on Task 1 was on the critical path, and the day you lost in Task 3 was noncritical—it was slack. Task 4 starts a day early in spite of Task 3 being delayed.

The paperwork got stuck in purchasing, and a one-day task dragged into three days. Task 4 is critical. That means you go into Task 5 running a day behind schedule, since Task 4 has eaten up the day you had gained in Task 1 and another one.

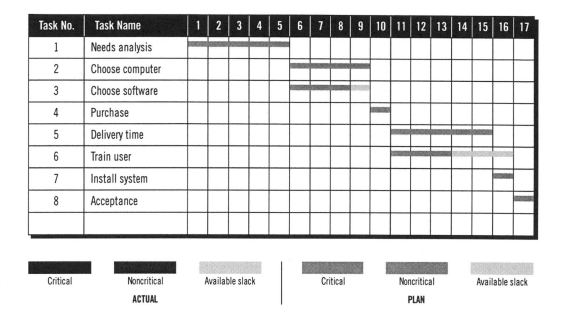

Figure 5.9 Tracking Gantt Chart

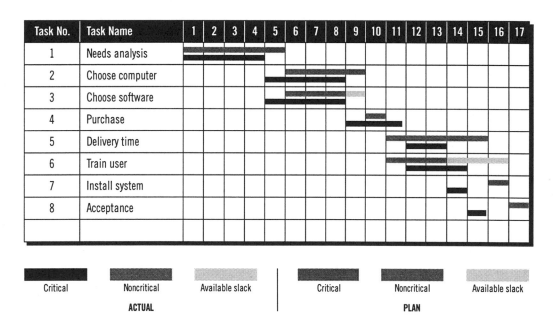

Figure 5.10 Tracking Gantt Chart Showing the Actual Project Time versus the Original Planned Time

Then you decided to crash Task 5 (you chose second-day air), reducing it to two days. The training started a day late, but the project finished early.

The value of this process is that at every stage you know what each early or late task means to the fate of the project as a whole. You can forecast a revised deadline at any time. You are empowered to act when you see the deadline slipping, and you save the project by understanding how to crash when needed.

Analyze a Project Gantt Chart

Your project is to install a company LAN system. You have been given the accompanying computer-created Gantt chart. Each job takes one full-time person. Team members possess all the necessary skills. Your job is to:
1. Determine the optimum team size, including the project manager.
2. Identify periods of resource slack.
3. Identify periods of resource overloads.
4. Determine if it is possible to level within slack.

ID	NAME	DURATION	June 6/11	6/18	6/25	7/2	July 7/9	7/16	7/23	7/30	August 8/6	8/13	8/20	8/27	September 9/3	9/10	9/17
1	Project management	15w															
2	Needs analysis	2w															
3	Specifications	2w															
4	Select server	1w															
5	Select software	3w															
6	Select cables	1w															
7	Purchasing	1w															
8	Manuals	2w															
9	Wire offices	3w															
10	Set up server	1w															
11	Develop training	3w															
12	Install software	1w															
13	Connect network	1w															
14	Train users	2w															
15	Test/debug	3w															
16	Acceptance	1w															

Project: Company LAN System

Critical	▬▬▬	Progress ———	Summary	◤▬▬◥
Noncritical	▒▒▒	Milestone ◆		

Answer Key

1. The first answer key shows the number of resources required each week of the project. The minimum is two, the maximum is four, and three is most common. Three is therefore the optimum team size.

2. Resource slack is available in the weeks of 6/11, 6/25, 7/16, 9/10, and 9/17, with one person each available those weeks (Resources = 2, Team Size =3).

3. Resource overload occurs in the weeks of 7/23 and 7/30, with the team being one person short in those weeks (Resources = 4, Team Size = 3).

4. One way to level within slack is shown in the second answer key. Assuming that Task 8, Manuals, can wait until the end of the project, you can shift that task so it takes place in the weeks of 9/10 and 9/17, when resource slack is available. This eliminates one week of resource overload. Second, you are delaying the start of Task 12, Install software, by one week, which eliminates the second week of resource overload.

First Answer Key

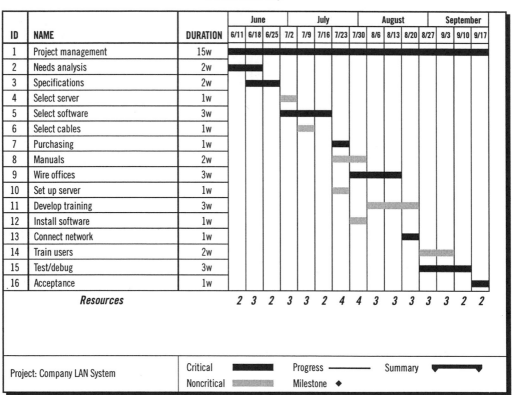

ID	NAME	DURATION	June 6/11	6/18	6/25	July 7/2	7/9	7/16	7/23	7/30	August 8/6	8/13	8/20	8/27	September 9/3	9/10	9/17
1	Project management	15w															
2	Needs analysis	2w															
3	Specifications	2w															
4	Select server	1w															
5	Select software	3w															
6	Select cables	1w															
7	Purchasing	1w															
8	Manuals	2w															
9	Wire offices	3w															
10	Set up server	1w															
11	Develop training	3w															
12	Install software	1w															
13	Connect network	1w															
14	Train users	2w															
15	Test/debug	3w															
16	Acceptance	1w															
Resources			*2*	*3*	*2*	*3*	*3*	*2*	*4*	*4*	*3*	*3*	*3*	*3*	*3*	*2*	*2*

Project: Company LAN System

Critical ▬▬▬   Progress ————   Summary ▼———▼
Noncritical ▒▒▒   Milestone ◆

Second Answer Key

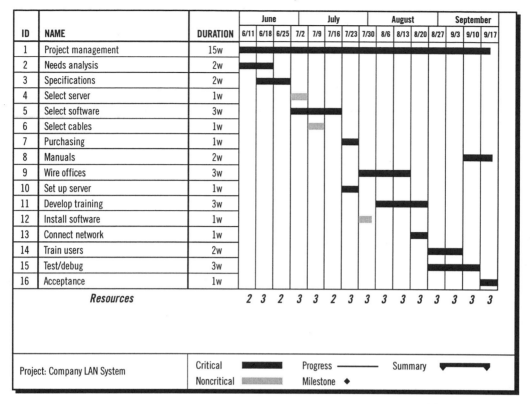

ID	NAME	DURATION	June 6/11	6/18	6/25	7/2	July 7/9	7/16	7/23	7/30	August 8/6	8/13	8/20	8/27	September 9/3	9/10	9/17
1	Project management	15w	████	████	████	████	████	████	████	████	████	████	████	████	████	████	
2	Needs analysis	2w	██														
3	Specifications	2w		██													
4	Select server	1w				▒											
5	Select software	3w				██	██										
6	Select cables	1w					▒										
7	Purchasing	1w							██								
8	Manuals	2w														██	
9	Wire offices	3w								██	██						
10	Set up server	1w							██								
11	Develop training	3w									██	██					
12	Install software	1w								▒							
13	Connect network	1w										██					
14	Train users	2w												██			
15	Test/debug	3w											██	██	██		
16	Acceptance	1w															██
	Resources		*2*	*3*	*2*	*3*	*3*	*2*	*3*	*3*	*3*	*3*	*3*	*3*	*3*	*3*	*3*

Project: Company LAN System

Critical ████ Progress ——— Summary ◥━━◤

Noncritical ▒▒▒▒ Milestone ◆

CHAPTER 6

How to Schedule Multiple Projects

"The basic problem I have is how to schedule the few people I have in the most efficient way to get all the work done," Patrick continued. "I can get any single project accomplished, no problem. But when I look at the mass of projects I need to get done in my department each year, I need to know how to schedule and plan the multiple project work effectively.

"Another key issue for me is priorities. Not all of the jobs you get have the same priority. Some have to be done, no fail. Others are important, but not at the same level. In the confusion and stress of trying to get it all done, sometimes you have a conflict with our priorities. This isn't too important, but it's easy and, besides, we're almost done. That is very important but difficult and far off in the future. And even worse, this one was vital, now it's optional, while that one used to be optional, and it's suddenly vital!"

Managing multiple independent project portfolios offers a variety of challenges. There is a strategy for managing them that builds on the single project management tools you have just covered.

DEFINITIONS

Here are the key terms you will need to know for this chapter.

Time-fixed projects are projects that have a fixed deadline. Time is always the driver.

Time-variable projects are projects with flexible deadlines. Either budget or performance criteria are the driver.

The *least resource* is the resource of which you have the smallest available quantity. When you schedule multiple resources across multiple projects, you may not have the same quantity of each resource.

Scheduling Issues for an Independent Project Portfolio

In putting together an effective plan for managing multiple projects in an independent project portfolio, a fondness for jigsaw puzzles helps. You have to fit the pieces carefully. It can get frustrating since you do not always have a picture on the box to follow.

Even though part of putting together a jigsaw puzzle is endless trial and error, you can apply strategies to make the job easier. For example, build the edge of the puzzle first. In scheduling for an independent project portfolio, you follow strategies to make the job easier, but the final elements require trial and error on your part.

Look at the strategic process for laying out your portfolio. There are five major steps to planning multiple projects.
1. Lay out time-fixed projects first.
2. Determine and schedule resource requirements.
3. Identify available resources for remaining projects.
4. Use least-resource scheduling to optimize production.
5. Fit the final schedule together.

Lay Out Time-Fixed Projects First

Patrick's production schedule involves a monthly magazine, a quarterly journal, three annual surveys, an annual meeting program, books, brochures, and special publications. The magazine, journal, annual surveys, and meeting programs are time-fixed projects, which means that time is their driver. Patrick must schedule these projects first, then fit the remaining work around the schedule.

A Note about Priority. Time-fixed projects must be done on time or not at all. Take a close look at the value and importance of your time-fixed projects. In some cases, the best strategy may be to cancel them altogether. If that is not appropriate, continue with the process described in this chapter.

One issue of the monthly magazine has already been scheduled. Now what happens when you copy that into a schedule for an entire calendar quarter? (See Figure 6.1.)

Summaries and milestones. The Gantt chart in Figure 6.1 was produced using a computer program, Microsoft Project in this case. You will notice a new symbol, called *a summary bar*, which is a long black bar with inverse triangles at each end (see Figure 6.2).

Remember that you can manage multiple projects using single project techniques, *because a project is a task, and a task is a project.* The summary bar shows multiple projects in the same Gantt chart, with the tasks within each project shown underneath it.

ID	NAME	DURATION	PREDECESSORS	RESOURCE NAMES
1	February 1997 issue	38.38 ed		1
2	Start issue	0d		1
3	Select manuscript and photos	5d	2	Kelly
4	Obtain editorials	4d	2	Patrick
5	Storyboard issue	2d	3	Kelly
6	Copyedit manuscripts	5d	4, 5	Kelly
7	Design/produce cover	2d	5	Rod
8	Place advertising	2d	7	Rod
9	Prepare turnover package	1d	6	Kelly
10	Create art and diagrams	4d	8, 9	DTP
11	Prepare distribution lists updates	1d	9	DTP
12	Create interior layouts	2d	10	Rod
13	Produce camera-ready art	2d	12	DTP
14	Proofread galleys	2d	13	Kelly
15	Coordinate with printer	6d	14	Rod [0.25]
16	Coordinate with manufacturing house	2d	11	Kelly [0.25]
17	Finish issue	0d	15, 16	
18	March 1997 issue	38.38 ed		
19	Start issue	0d		
20	Select manuscript and photos	5d	19	Justin
21	Obtain editorials	4d	19	Patrick
22	Storyboard issue	2d	20	Justin
23	Copyedit manuscripts	5d	21, 22	Justin
24	Design/produce cover	2d	22	Rod
25	Place advertising	2d	24	rod
26	Prepare turnover package	1d	23	Justin
27	Create art and diagrams	4d	25, 26	DTP
28	Prepare distribution lists updates	1d	26	DTP
29	Create interior layouts	2d	27	Rod
30	Produce camera-ready art	2d	29	DTP
31	Proofread galleys	2d	30	Justin
32	Coordinate with printer	6d	31	Rod [0.25]
33	Coordinate with manufacturing house	2d	28	Justin [0.25]
34	Finish issue	0d	32, 33	
35	April 1997 issue	38.38 ed		
36	Start issue	0d		
37	Select manuscript and photos	5d	36	Kelly
38	Obtain editorials	4d	36	Patrick
39	Storyboard issue	2d	37, 38	Kelly
40	Copyedit manuscripts	5d	38, 39	Kelly
41	Design/produce cover	2d	39	Rod
42	Place advertising	2d	41	Rod
43	Prepare turnover package	1d	40	Kelly
44	Create art and diagrams	4d	42, 43	DTP
45	Prepare distribution lists updates	1d	43	DTP
46	Create interior layouts	2d	44	Rod
47	Produce camera-ready art	2d	46	DTP
48	Proofread galleys	2d	47	Kelly
49	Coordinate with printer	6d	48	Rod [0.25]
50	Coordinate with manufacturing house	2d	45	Justin [0.25]
51	Finish issue	0d	49, 50	
52	1st Quarter Journal	95.38 ed		
53	Start issue	0d		
54	Select articles	3d	53	Patrick
55	Send articles to reviewers	1d	54	Patrick
56	Receive reviewer comment	30d	55	
57	Final article selection	2d	56	Patrick
58	Copyedit manuscripts	10d	57	Patrick
59	Produce cover	2d	57	Rod
60	Typeset and produce interior	4d	58	DTP
61	Create charts/diagrams	5d	58	DTP
62	Prepare camera-ready art	2d	60, 61	DTP
63	Proofread galleys	3d	62	Patrick
64	Coordinate with printer	5d	63	Rod [0.25]
65	Update manufacturing list	1d	58	Patrick
66	Coordinate with manufacturing house	2d	65	Partrick [0.25]
67	Mail issue	0d	64, 66	

Project:
Date: 5/8/96

Critical ▬▬▬ Noncritical ▧▧▧ Progress ——— Milestone ◆ Summary ▼▬▼

Figure 6.1 A Sample Portfolio Gantt Chart

How to Schedule Multiple Projects

Figure 6.2 A Summary Bar

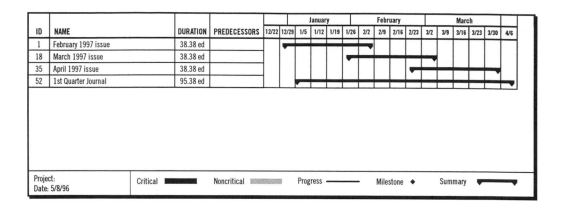

ID	NAME	DURATION	PREDECESSORS	January						February				March				
				12/22	12/29	1/5	1/12	1/19	1/26	2/2	2/9	2/16	2/23	3/2	3/9	3/16	3/23	3/30	4/6
1	February 1997 issue	38.38 ed																
18	March 1997 issue	38.38 ed																
35	April 1997 issue	38.38 ed																
52	1st Quarter Journal	95.38 ed																

Project:
Date: 5/8/96

Critical ▬▬ Noncritical ▨▨ Progress —— Milestone ◆ Summary ▬◥

Figure 6.3 Portfolio Gantt Chart

The other symbol introduced in Figure 6.1 is the diamond (◆), called a milestone. A milestone is a task that takes zero time to complete. Start issue, Task 2 on the schedule, is a milestone. Milestones are located wherever they help clarify a schedule. Important checkpoints and events usually deserve a milestone.

Using computer software can also show you the projects together on the same chart (see Figure 6.3). You may also do this on a magnetic scheduling board, graph paper, or anywhere else you would display a Gantt chart of all your projects.

Determine and Schedule Resource Requirements

Once you have all the time-fixed projects in your schedule, go through a staff-assignment process identical to the one followed for a single project. You have the option to do this manually or by computer. The resource Gantt charts in figures 6.4–6.8 were created on the computer. You will notice that on the portfolio Gantt chart, there is a resource name assignment for each task. (The numbers in brackets, e.g., Rod [0.25], denotes a part-time job. Rod works one-quarter time on that task during that period.)

Expect some trial and error in this process. For the sample publishing project, first assign the jobs to people on our team for a single issue of the magazine, and then duplicate the assignments for the other issues. You will see that this will not work because the time to produce each issue is more than a month. To distribute the issues on time, you will have to overlap the schedule, which creates staff conflicts—periods of resource overload. Consider several possibilities of leveling and reassigning. Finally, settle on having your two editors, Kelly and Justin, alternate issues.

ID	NAME	DURATION	PREDECESSORS	12/22	12/29	1/5	1/12	1/19	1/26	2/2	2/9	2/16	2/23	3/2	3/9	3/16	3/23	3/30	4/6
4	Obtain editorials	4d	2		▨														
21	Obtain editorials	4d	19						▨										
38	Obtain editorials	4d	36									▨							
54	Select articles	3d	53			▨													
55	Send articles to reviewers	1d	54			▮													
57	Final article selection	2d	56										▨						
58	Copyedit manuscripts	10d	57											▨▨▨					
63	Proofread galleys	3d	62														■		
65	Update mailing list	1d	58												▮				
66	Coordinate with mailing house	2d	65												▨				

				January				February				March			

Project:		Critical ▬▬▬	Noncritical ▨▨▨	Progress ———	Milestone ◆	Summary ▬▬▶
Date: 5/8/96						

Figure 6.4   Resource Gantt Chart for Patrick

Fitting in the first quarter issue of the research journal is even more challenging. One advantage you have is that the task, Receive reviewer comments, is a lag activity—no work is involved. Still, you will have to assign the editorial responsibility to Patrick, the department head, to schedule the work.

Once all the tasks are assigned, you may produce *resource Gantt charts* for each member of the team (see figures 6.4–6.8).

Identify Available Resources for Remaining Projects

When you examine the individual resource Gantt charts, it is obvious that doing our three monthly issues and one quarterly journal is not a full-time commitment for the department. You can do more work. The question is, how much more?

Resource Gantt charts. You may answer this question by creating resource time charts, either using a project management software package or working manually. You calculated resource requirements in Chapter 5. The program prints out a *resource time chart* listing project and task commitments for each person for each work day in the quarter (see Figure 6.9).

Remember, our work team consists of:

- Patrick, department head and backup editor, forty hours per week availability
- Kelly, editor, forty hours per week availability
- Justin, editor, forty hours per week availability
- Rod, graphic designer, forty hours per week availability
- two staff members, desktop publishing (DTP), eighty hours per week availability.

Time availability grid. A time availability grid shows the noncommitted time for each member of our team each week, and totals the hours at the bottom of the page. To make the grid, simply add the number of unscheduled hours in each week on the resource time chart.

Figure 6.5 Resource Gantt Chart for Kelly

ID	NAME	DURATION	PREDECESSORS
3	Select manuscripts and photos	5d	2
5	Storyboard issue	2d	3
6	Copyedit manuscripts	5d	4, 5
9	Prepare turnover package	1d	6
14	Proofread galleys	2d	13
16	Coordinate with mailing house	2d	11
37	Select manuscripts and photos	5d	36
39	Storyboard issue	2d	37, 38
40	Copyedit manuscripts	5d	38, 39
43	Prepare turnover package	1d	40
48	Proofread galleys	2d	47

Project: Date: 5/8/96

Critical ■■■■■ Noncritical ▨▨▨▨ Progress ——— Milestone ◆ Summary ▼——▼

Figure 6.5 Resource Gantt Chart for Kelly

ID	NAME	DURATION	PREDECESSORS
20	Select manuscripts and photos	5d	19
22	Storyboard issue	2d	20
23	Copyedit manuscripts	5d	21, 22
26	Prepare turnover package	1d	23
31	Proofread galleys	2d	30
33	Coordinate with mailing house	2d	28
50	Coordinate with mailing house	2d	45

Project: Date: 5/8/96

Critical ■■■■■ Noncritical ▨▨▨▨ Progress ——— Milestone ◆ Summary ▼——▼

Figure 6.6 Resource Gantt Chart for Justin

Kelly has 356 available hours (a little less than nine weeks); Justin has 472 hours (nearly twelve weeks); Rod has 394 hours (nearly ten weeks); DTP has 928 hours (slightly over twenty-three weeks); and Patrick has 340 hours (a little over eight weeks).

Strategic reserve time. Staff members have to allow time for administrative duties first. Assume that this averages two hours a week for everyone but Patrick. For Patrick, it averages sixteen hours a week, and if he does not have sixteen hours available in one week, it rolls into next week. With the exception of Patrick, team members are available forty-two hours a week. This is close enough. When you allocate someone

Figure 6.7 Resource Gantt Chart for Rod

ID	NAME	DURATION	PREDECESSORS	12/29	1/5	1/12	1/19	1/26	2/2	2/9	2/16	2/23	3/2	3/9	3/16	3/23	3/30	4/6	4/13
7	Design/produce cover	2d	5	▧															
8	Place advertising	2d	7		▧														
12	Create interior layouts	2d	10				▧												
15	Coordinate with printer	6d	14						▧▧										
24	Design/produce cover	2d	22							▧									
25	Place advertising	2d	24							▧									
29	Create interior layouts	2d	27									▧							
32	Coordinate with printer	6d	31									▧▧							
41	Design/produce cover	2d	29											▧					
42	Place advertising	2d	41											▧					
46	Create interior layouts	2d	44												▧				
49	Coordinate with printer	6d	48													▧▧			
59	Produce cover	2d	57									▧							
64	Coordinate with printer	5d	63														▰▰		

Project:
Date: 5/8/96

Critical ▰▰▰▰ Noncritical ▧▧▧▧ Progress ──── Milestone ◆ Summary ▼──▼

Figure 6.8 Resource Gantt Chart for Desktop Publishing Department

ID	NAME	DURATION	PREDECESSORS	12/29	1/5	1/12	1/19	1/26	2/2	2/9	2/16	2/23	3/2	3/9	3/16	3/23	3/30	4/6	4/13
10	Create art and diagrams	4d	8, 9			▧▧													
11	Prepare distribution list updates	1d	9			▧													
13	Produce camera-ready art	2d	12					▧											
27	Create art and diagrams	4d	25, 26							▧▧									
28	Prepare distribution list updates	1d	26							▧									
30	Produce camera-ready art	2d	29									▧							
44	Create art and diagrams	4d	42, 43											▧▧					
45	Prepare distribution list updates	1d	43											▧					
47	Produce camera-ready art	2d	46												▧				
60	Typeset and produce interior	4d	58												▰▰				
61	Create charts and diagrams	5d	58												▧▧				
62	Produce camera-ready art	2d	60, 61													▪			

Project:
Date: 5/8/96

Critical ▰▰▰▰ Noncritical ▧▧▧▧ Progress ──── Milestone ◆ Summary ▼──▼

Figure 6.8 Resource Gantt Chart for Desktop Publishing Department

five days to do a job, you assume that they will not be working every minute of every day on the project. With personal time-management skills, the team should be able to handle slight excess without a problem.

How to Schedule Multiple Projects

Resource Time Chart — First Quarter

Weeks of December 29 – January 26

ID	NAME	Dec 29							Jan 5							Jan 12							Jan 19							Jan 26						
		S	M	T	W	T	F	S	S	M	T	W	T	F	S	S	M	T	W	T	F	S	S	M	T	W	T	F	S	S	M	T	W	T	F	S
1	Kelly		8h	8h	8h	8h				8h	8h	8h	8h	8h			8h	8h	8h	8h				2h	2h									8h	8h	
2	Justin																														8h	8h	8h	8h	8h	
3	Rod					8h	8h										8h	8h									8h	8h								2h
4	DTP																				16h			8h	8h	8h					8h	8h				
5	Patrick		8h	8h	8h	8h				8h	8h	8h	8h																		8h	8h	8h	8h		

Weeks of February 2 – March 2

ID	NAME	Feb 2							Feb 9							Feb 16							Feb 23							Mar 2						
		S	M	T	W	T	F	S	S	M	T	W	T	F	S	S	M	T	W	T	F	S	S	M	T	W	T	F	S	S	M	T	W	T	F	S
1	Kelly																							8h	8h	8h	8h	8h			8h	8h	8h	8h	8h	
2	Justin		8h	8h	8h	8h	8h			8h	8h	8h		2h			2h								8h	8h										
3	Rod		2h	2h	2h	2h	2h			8h	8h	8h	8h							8h	8h			8h	8h			2h			2h	2h	2h	2h	2h	
4	DTP												8h	8h			8h	8h	8h					8h	8h											
5	Patrick																				8h			8h	8h	8h	8h	8h			8h	8h	8h	8h	8h	

Weeks of March 9 – April 6

ID	NAME	Mar 9							Mar 16							Mar 23							Mar 30							Apr 6						
		S	M	T	W	T	F	S	S	M	T	W	T	F	S	S	M	T	W	T	F	S	S	M	T	W	T	F	S	S	M	T	W	T	F	S
1	Kelly		8h	8h	8h													8h	8h																	
2	Justin				2h					2h																										
3	Rod		8h	8h	8h	8h							8h	8h							2h			2h	2h	2h	2h	4h			2h	2h	2h	2h		
4	DTP					8h	8h			16h	16h	16h	8h	8h			16h	16h	8h	8h	8h			8h												
5	Patrick		8h	8h	8h	8h	8h			8h	2h	2h												8h	8h	8h										

Figure 6.9 Resource Time Chart for Each Employee for Each Workday during the First Quarter

Second, the schedule as drawn makes no allowance for things going wrong. Allow four hours a week for catch-up time. Since there are not four available hours in every week, you will save it and add it later.

Tip! When scheduling limited people across multiple projects, add formal catch-up time to their schedules. If you do not, anything that goes wrong, whether it is the fault of the team member or not, bumps every subsequent task of that team member. This can quickly spiral into disaster.

Next, make allowance for those pesky special projects that management keeps putting into our schedule (see the introduction to Patrick's problem). How do you figure what is a safe allowance? In this case, you would turn to historical data. On average, how many of these special projects materialize in a quarter? How long do

Week of:	Kelly	Justin	Rod	DTP (2)	Patrick
12/29	8	40	40	80	8
1/5	0	40	24	64	8
1/12	8	40	24	64	40
1/19	36	40	24	56	40
1/26	24	0	38	64	8
2/2	40	0	30	80	40
2/9	40	14	8	64	40
2/16	40	38	24	56	32
2/23	0	24	22	64	0
3/2	0	40	30	80	0
3/9	16	38	8	64	0
3/16	40	38	24	16	28
3/23	24	40	38	24	40
3/30	40	40	28	72	16
4/6	40	40	32	80	40
TOTALS	356	472	394	928	340

Figure 6.10   Time Availability Grid for First Quarter 1997

they take? You will see that you have built a special project allowance into everyone's schedule except Patrick's. As department head, he already has enough to do.

When you take the total of these additional work requirements from the available time, you are left with the strategic reserve time (SRT) for each team member. (Notice the similarity of this process to the one used for Carolyn's individual project in Chapter 2.)

The SRT is what you have available for other important long-range work that Patrick wants the department to do: produce technical management books and upgrade technology and systems to improve productivity.

Use Least-Resource Scheduling to Optimize Production

Knowing the SRT of each of your team members is the critical first step for optimizing the total productivity of your work team. Now, you have to figure the best way to fit additional work into the time and resources you have available.

That takes us back to our jigsaw-puzzle analogy. One strategy for putting together your jigsaw puzzle is to put together the edge pieces first, then fit the remaining pieces inside. The edge in this case involves the concept of least-resource scheduling.

Week of:	Avail.	Admin.	Catch-Up	Spec. Proj.	Total	SRT
12/29	8	2	0	0	2	6
1/5	0	2	0	0	2	-2
1/12	8	2	0	0	2	6
1/19	36	2	16	16	34	2
1/26	24	2	4	16	22	2
2/2	40	2	4	8	14	26
2/9	40	2	4	0	6	34
2/16	40	2	4	24	30	10
2/23	0	2	0	0	2	-2
3/2	0	2	0	0	2	-2
3/9	16	2	12	0	14	2
3/16	40	2	4	16	22	18
3/23	24	2	4	16	22	2
3/30	40	2	4	8	14	26
4/6	40	2	4	0	6	34
TOTALS	356	30	60	104	194	162

Figure 6.11   Kelly Strategic Reserve Time First Quarter 1997

One thing you notice about Patrick's department is that it is lopsided. Look at the range of available time for members of this team:

■ Patrick: 50 hours
■ Kelly: 162 hours
■ Justin: 262 hours
■ Rod: 152 hours
■ DTP: 556 hours.

Least-resource scheduling.   To understand the concept of least-resource scheduling, imagine that you run a construction company. Your independent project portfolio consists of the various buildings you have contracted to build. Your resources involve both people and equipment.

Imagine you only own one backhoe. You need the backhoe for two weeks on each project. No matter what, your theoretical best-case ability is limited to twenty-six buildings per year. No matter how many cranes, dump trucks, or people you employ, the single backhoe sets the speed limit for production.

That twenty-six building production limit is generous. The reality is that the backhoe will need maintenance, weather will interfere, and so on. The real pro-

Week of:	Avail.	Admin.	Catch-Up	Spec. Proj.	Total	SRT
12/29	40	2	4	16	22	18
1/5	40	2	4	16	22	18
1/12	40	2	4	8	14	26
1/19	40	2	4	0	6	34
1/26	0	2	0	0	2	−2
2/2	0	2	0	0	2	−2
2/9	14	2	12	0	14	0
2/16	38	2	4	16	22	16
2/23	24	2	4	16	22	2
3/2	40	2	4	8	14	26
3/9	38	2	4	0	6	32
3/16	38	2	4	16	22	16
3/23	40	2	4	16	22	18
3/30	40	2	4	8	14	26
4/6	40	2	4	0	6	34
TOTALS	472	30	60	120	210	262

Figure 6.12   Justin Strategic Reserve Time First Quarter 1997

duction will be somewhat less. If you are going to get the most total production out of your resources, you have to make sure you do not waste any backhoe time.

You would naturally want to schedule the backhoe first, to make sure it is used optimally. Then you fit the other resources around the backhoe's schedule—*in the order of least to most available*—to optimize production. Having a few dump trucks sitting around the yard unused on a given week is not necessarily wasteful if dump trucks are your most available resource.

When your resources are not exactly in balance, and they usually are not, you cannot help but have some excess. Make sure the excess is in the most available resource, not the least.

Determining the Least Resource

At first glance, Rod is the least resource on our team, because he has the fewest number of SRT hours available. That is usually not enough evidence to make a final decision.

One of the reasons for resource inequality on a project team is that people (and other resources) have different abilities and functions, and these are not always interchangeable.

Week of:	Avail.	Admin.	Catch-Up	Spec. Proj.	Total	SRT
12/29	40	2	4	0	6	34
1/5	24	2	4	0	6	18
1/12	24	2	4	0	6	18
1/19	24	2	4	16	22	2
1/26	38	2	4	16	22	16
2/2	30	2	4	0	6	24
2/9	8	2	4	0	6	2
2/16	24	2	4	16	22	2
2/23	22	2	4	16	22	0
3/2	30	2	4	24	30	0
3/9	8	2	4	0	6	2
3/16	24	2	4	16	22	2
3/23	38	2	4	24	30	8
3/30	28	2	4	0	6	22
4/6	32	2	4	24	30	2
TOTALS	394	30	60	152	242	152

Figure 6.13   Rod Strategic Reserve Time First Quarter 1997

If all the team members have the same skills, assigning people in the order of fewest SRT hours to most SRT hours would be enough.

On our team, you have three people with editorial skills, one person with graphic design skills, and two people with desktop publishing skills, and they are not interchangeable. When planning least resources, you have to consider non-interchangeable skills. In fact, what you really have is:

- Editorial: 474 hours
- Graphics: 152 hours
- DTP: 556 hours.

Even this analysis, which still leaves Rod as the least resource, is not enough to be certain. The projects you are trying to put into place are books, not magazines. In our situation, our books—dry, technical guides used as industry reference materials—tend to use a standard interior design. They require less graphic design time than the magazines. The DTP team performs most of the production work, except for the cover. The books are heavy in editorial requirements, too. Imagine that each book project requires eighty hours of editorial work, forty hours of desktop publishing, and only sixteen hours of graphic design work. You would need to look at availability in terms of number of projects, not number of hours. You would end up with:

Week of:	Avail.	Admin.	Catch-Up	Spec. Proj.	Total	SRT
12/29	80	4	8	0	12	68
1/5	64	4	8	0	12	52
1/12	64	4	8	0	12	52
1/19	56	4	8	0	12	44
1/26	64	4	8	48	60	4
2/2	80	4	8	0	12	68
2/9	64	4	8	0	12	52
2/16	56	4	8	0	12	44
2/23	64	4	8	0	12	52
3/2	80	4	8	48	60	20
3/9	64	4	8	48	60	4
3/16	16	4	8	0	12	4
3/23	24	4	8	0	12	12
3/30	72	4	8	48	60	12
4/6	80	4	8	0	12	68
TOTALS	928	60	120	192	372	556

Figure 6.14   Desktop Publishing Strategic Reserve Time First Quarter 1997

- Editorial: 6 projects
- Graphics: 9.5 projects
- DTP: 14 projects.

Notice that this would make Editorial, not Graphics, the least resource. Our theoretical, best-case book-publishing capacity is six projects for this quarter.

Think strategically. Always use project capacity, not just hours or number of resources, in determining which is your least resource.

Capacity Management for the Least Resource

You are not finished. If a book project requires eighty hours of editorial commitment, and Patrick only has fifty hours left for the entire quarter, you really should not count him as available for editorial work. That cuts editorial time to 424 hours, or 5.3 books, which you must round down to five (you cannot do a partial book), with twenty-four hours of editorial time uncommitted for the quarter.

Now look at Kelly and Justin, who will edit all our books. Kelly has 162 hours, which is two books with two hours left over, and Justin has 262 hours, which is three books, with twenty-two hours remaining. In Kelly's case, scheduling her work for a three-month period with only a total safety margin of two hours is ludicrous.

Week of:	Avail.	Admin.	Catch-Up	Spec. Proj.	Total	SRT
12/29	8	8	0	0	8	0
1/5	8	8	0	0	8	0
1/12	40	32	8	0	40	0
1/19	40	16	8	0	24	16
1/26	8	8	0	0	8	0
2/2	40	24	8	0	32	8
2/9	40	16	8	0	24	16
2/16	32	16	0	0	16	16
2/23	0	2	0	0	2	–2
3/2	0	2	0	0	2	–2
3/9	0	2	0	0	2	–2
3/16	28	28	0	0	28	0
3/23	40	36	4	0	40	0
3/30	16	16	0	0	16	0
4/6	40	16	24	0	40	0
TOTALS	340	230	60	0	290	50

Figure 6.15   Patrick Strategic Reserve Time First Quarter 1997

However, no one says that every book project must be started and finished within the same quarter. Schedule her for three books over six months, which would be 1.5 books in this quarter, with forty-two hours left over.

This is an ambitious schedule but not absurd. You have a reasonable margin in editorial work, and you will end up producing nine books in six months while keeping up with normal production.

Scheduling Excess Resources

Rod's graphics schedule now has to allow for 4.5 projects at sixteen hours per project or seventy-two hours for the quarter, leaving eighty hours or two full weeks currently unallocated over a three-month period. Depending on surprises, problems, sick leave, and other emergencies, this may not be an excessive allowance; it is less than three days per month. You may want to add that into catch-up and emergency time and feel you have scheduled well enough. If you want to avoid the possibility of waste, identify some general projects that need to be done but do not have a specific deadline (organize the art files, check out other printers, and so on), and assign those to Rod. He can do as much of them as possible, and if emergencies crop up, nothing is lost.

The more serious problem is in DTP. You had 556 unscheduled hours. You subtract 4.5 projects at forty hours per project (180 hours), leaving 376 hours, which is nearly 9.5 weeks! You cannot allow that sort of waste in a well-run department. Fortunately, you can avoid it.

Sometimes you overlook support staff in a department. Because support staff members are sometimes younger or less educated, they are sometimes not thought of as professional. Nevertheless, support staff members are frequently looking for the opportunity to develop themselves and advance, or, even if advancement is not their ambition, they often want more interesting and varied work to do.

Here is an opportunity for some creative win/win thinking. Look at some ways you can use those 9.5 weeks effectively.

■ Arrange training for them. The DTP people may be able to develop graphic design and editorial skills. This might qualify them for promotions or at least identify more challenging work, take the burden off other staff, and increase total productivity.

■ Assign them to improve productivity. They probably know the hardware and software capabilities better than anyone else. Put them in charge of projects to use all the software tools and functions and to train the rest of the department in how to improve productivity.

■ Trade with other departments. Your excess capacity may be just what another department needs, and it may have excess capacity that would help solve your problems. Talk to other managers to evaluate possibilities.

Think strategically. In planning work for a team, build from the scarcest resources to the most available, and use your surplus resources for long-term projects that improve productivity.

Fit the Final Schedule Together

Now, return to the jigsaw puzzle. You have the existing schedule; you need to allow for the various administrative, catch-up, and emergency project issues. You want to produce 4.5 books; and you want to assign some productivity-improvement projects to the DTP department (and one for Rod). All the earlier steps build the puzzle frame. Put together the rest of the puzzle, using trial and error.

This is a time-consuming process with some frustration attached. One shortcut is to ask team members to plan their own time around their time-fixed projects, enter the data, and resolve final conflicts. Another shortcut is the payoff from the learning curve, the more scheduling you do, the easier it gets.

Jigsaw Puzzle Scheduling

Take a close look at the first month of our quarter. You are doing the entire February issue, starting the March issue late in the month, and starting the first-quarter journal issue. (Notice that the task, Receive reviewer comment, is a lag activity.)

ID	NAME	DURATION	PREDECESSORS	RESOURCE NAMES
1	February 1997 issue	38.38 ed		1
2	Start issue	0d		1
3	Select manuscript and photos	5d	2	Kelly
4	Obtain editorials	4d	2	Patrick
5	Storyboard issue	2d	3	Kelly
6	Copyedit manuscripts	5d	4, 5	Kelly
7	Design/produce cover	2d	5	Rod
8	Place advertising	2d	7	Rod
9	Prepare turnover package	1d	6	Kelly
10	Create art and diagrams	4d	8, 9	DTP
11	Prepare distribution lists updates	1d	9	DTP
12	Create interior layouts	2d	10	Rod
13	Produce camera-ready art	2d	12	DTP
14	Proofread galleys	2d	13	Kelly
15	Coordinate with printer	6d	14	Rod [0.25]
16	Coordinate with mailing house	2d	11	Kelly [0.25]
17	Finish issue	0d	15, 16	
18	March 1997 issue	38.38 ed		
19	Start issue	0d		
20	Select manuscript and photos	5d	19	Justin
21	Obtain editorials	4d	19	Patrick
22	Storyboard issue	2d	20	Justin
23	Copyedit manuscripts	5d	21, 22	Justin
24	1st Quarter Journal	95.38 ed		
25	Start issue	0d		
26	Select articles	3d	25	Patrick
27	Send articles to reviewers	1d	26	Patrick
28	Receive reviewer comment	30d	27	

Project:
Date: 5/8/96

Critical █████ Noncritical ░░░░░ Progress ——— Milestone ◆ Summary ▼━━━▼

Here is Kelly's resource Gantt chart, showing her part of the month's schedule.

ID	NAME	DURATION	PREDECESSORS	RESOURCE NAMES
3	Select manuscript and photos	5d	2	Kelly
5	Storyboard issue	2d	3	Kelly
6	Copyedit manuscripts	5d	4, 5	Kelly
9	Prepare turnover package	1d	6	Kelly
14	Proofread galleys	2d	13	Kelly
16	Coordinate with mailing house	2d	11	Kelly [0.25]

Project:
Date: 5/8/96

Critical ▬▬ Noncritical ░░░ Progress ——— Milestone ◆ Summary ▼━━▼

And here is Kelly's strategic reserve time chart for January.

Week of:	Avail.	Admin.	Catch-Up	Spec. Proj.	Total	SRT
12/29	8	2	0	0	2	6
1/5	0	2	0	0	2	−2
1/12	8	2	0	0	2	6
1/19	36	2	16	16	34	2
1/26	24	2	4	16	22	2
TOTALS	76	10	20	32	62	14

1. Fit her additional responsibilities into her schedule.

2. Can she even begin work on a book project this month?

How to Schedule Multiple Projects

Answer Key

Answer to question 1: More than one answer may be possible. Here is one version of her complete schedule.

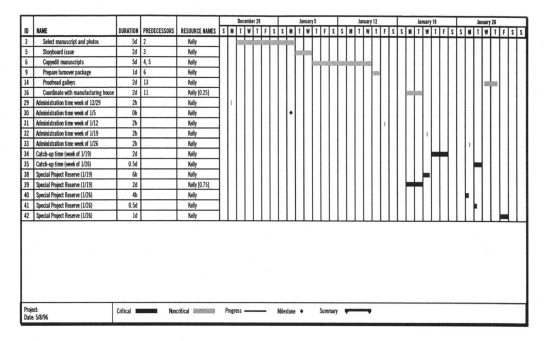

ID	NAME	DURATION	PREDECESSORS	RESOURCE NAMES	December 29	January 5	January 12	January 19	January 26
3	Select manuscript and photos	5d	2	Kelly					
5	Storyboard issue	2d	3	Kelly					
6	Copyedit manuscripts	5d	4, 5	Kelly					
9	Prepare turnover package	1d	6	Kelly					
14	Proofread galleys	2d	13	Kelly					
16	Coordinate with manufacturing house	2d	11	Kelly [0.25]					
29	Administration time week of 12/29	2h		Kelly					
30	Administration time week of 1/5	0h		Kelly					
31	Administration time week of 1/12	2h		Kelly					
32	Administration time week of 1/19	2h		Kelly					
33	Administration time week of 1/26	2h		Kelly					
34	Catch-up time (week of 1/19)	2d		Kelly					
35	Catch-up time (week of 1/26)	0.5d		Kelly					
38	Special Project Reserve (1/19)	6h		Kelly					
39	Special Project Reserve (1/19)	2d		Kelly [0.75]					
40	Special Project Reserve (1/26)	4h		Kelly					
41	Special Project Reserve (1/26)	0.5d		Kelly					
42	Special Project Reserve (1/26)	1d		Kelly					

Project:
Date: 5/8/96

Critical ▬▬▬   Noncritical ▨▨▨   Progress ▬▬▬   Milestone ◆   Summary ▼▬▬▬▼

In producing this on the computer, each time you started and stopped a task (because something else was on her schedule), you had to start a new task line. Task 30, Administration time week of 1/5, is 0 hours, not 2, because she is already scheduled for 40 that week. As we pointed out earlier in this chapter, you are not really going to allow for this time; you simply expect Kelly to be efficient enough to make up two hours or work overtime. (She is probably an exempt employee, and you do not have to pay for her overtime anyway.)

Answer to question 2: No. Justin, on the other hand, could easily do one.

The Juggler's Guide to Managing Multiple Projects

CHAPTER 7

How to Manage Multiple Projects in an Independent Portfolio

Now that Patrick has put together a complete schedule for the multiple projects in his portfolio, he has a set of new concerns:

- *How realistic is this schedule?*
- *How do I make sure that the work is done according to the schedule?*
- *How do I deal with management coming up with more special projects than I planned?*
- *How do I communicate the schedule to members of my team and to my own management?*
- *What do I do when a team member see the priorities differently—putting continued effort into a marginal project?*
- *What kind of warning do I get when things go wrong?*

Managing a project is different from planning it, and in this chapter you will look at issues of managing your project portfolio once it has been planned and scheduled.

DEFINITIONS

Here are the key terms you will need to understand in this chapter.

Portfolio constraints are the triple constraints of the entire portfolio, as distinct from the constraints of the individual projects within the portfolio.

SMART is an acronym for specific, measurable, agreed-upon (or accountable), realistic, and time-specific. Comparing your goals to this acronym is a standard method of deciding whether your goals are properly drawn.

THE ART OF MANAGING MULTIPLE PROJECT PORTFOLIOS IN ORGANIZATIONS

A large part of this book focuses on the art of planning; this is no accident. The Five P's—*prior planning prevents poor performance*—is the most important idea you can use to get the job done. Nothing can prevent all problems, but good planning can at least reduce them and put you more in control.

Many of your problems as a manager of multiple projects happen for two reasons: 1) projects take place within organizations, and, 2) projects have customers. Both organizations and customers consist of people. People have different interests, goals, and styles. People do not as a rule check their humanity at the door when they punch the time clock, which means that projects tend to have a political and emotional agenda, as well as a specific technical goal. Although the political aspects of projects may be a source of frustration (and of occasional despair), you must develop strategies and tactics to deal with them.

Project managers need to be management generalists. In addition to the formal work of project management, you will be involved in all the other duties of managers as well: supervision, leadership, office politics, reports, meetings, and so on.

Good planning is at the core of project management success, both for single and multiple projects. It is not the only thing you must worry about. Look at why some projects succeed and others fail.

Why Some Projects Fail ...

■ Lack of project manager authority: "I must be a mushroom. They keep me in the dark, feed me mushroom food, and then they can me."
■ Lack of team participation: "If workers were smart, they'd be managers. Why ask them anything? After all, I'm the boss."
■ Poor reporting: "Reports are just a lot of useless paperwork and an irrelevant requirement of management. I fill out the form and then forget the form."
■ Lack of people skills: "I don't thank people just for doing a good job. Doing a good job is what they get paid for."
■ Unrealistic goals and schedules: "Your mission, should you decide to accept it ... if caught or killed, the Secretary will disavow any knowledge ... "

... and Others Succeed

■ Committed teamwork:

> If anything goes bad, I did it. If anything goes semi-good, then we did it. If anything goes real good, then you did it. That's all it takes to get people to win football games.

Paul "Bear" Bryant

■ SMART goals with real consensus: Specific, Measurable, Agreed-upon, Realistic, and Time-Specific.

■ Use of project management tools as a means, not an end: "We have 238 pages of charts and graphs and still do not have a clue!"

YOUR ROLE AS PROJECT PORTFOLIO MANAGER

Whenever you are in a management role, you have some power, and you also have some limits on that power. When you manage multiple projects, you often have others responsible for the management of the individual projects inside your portfolio. You must delegate some parts of your responsibility and authority to others. As with other elements of managing your project, you should think about the power you have, the power you need, and the power you are willing to give to the individual project managers within your team.

You can use a worksheet to organize your thinking on this important issue; it serves as the exercise that ends this chapter. Growth and improvement are almost always possible. You may find the exercise somewhat depressing when you realize how little real authority you have. Remember that real power in organizations is often more informal than formal, and you can follow strategies of personal development that will yield greater effectiveness and control. Ways by which you can ethically and effectively gain more power to accomplish results include the following.

■ Personal assertiveness: Strong self-esteem is a project management skill. If you are given what seems to be an impossible project assignment, you have to say something about it. If the information you have is not sufficient, you have to ask for additional information. If you do not have assertiveness and self-esteem, others are likely to walk on you.

■ Track record of accomplishment: "Nothing succeeds like success," the old saying goes, and this is true of project managers. Each time you achieve your goal and each time you get the job done when others could not, you gain power and influence proportional to the respect your accomplishment earned. The best of all political skills is earning a reputation for outstanding work.

■ Knowledge and insight: When you earn a reputation for knowing what you are talking about, you gain power and influence. Commit yourself to learning more about your field, organization, customers, and projects.

■ Relationships: Some people say, "It is not what you know, it is who you know." Actually, it is both what you know and who you know. The ability to build good professional relationships with people above you, below you, and at the same level in the organization and throughout your industry is an important skill that yields influence and power.

■ Initiative: Take the initiative on the projects in your portfolio: make decisions; take intelligent risks. Initiative is one of the ingredients of good management everywhere.

■ People skills: The ability to work and play well with others, which you remember so well from your childhood report cards, is still an important element in adulthood, especially as project managers.

■ Communications skills: "If you don't ask, you don't get." Communication is part of all these power issues. The art of communication involves the ability to articulate your goals and desires, put them across in persuasive and positive language, and get your message understood. You must be understood before you can be accepted or have others to agree with you.

■ Understanding: What is the real goal of the project? Who are the key players, and what do they want? The ability to put yourself in others' shoes and understand the reasons for the project, the goals and missions of the organization in which you work, the limitations and concerns faced by your managers and your team members, and the motivations of others—these are powerful tools to improve your effectiveness.

THE TRIPLE CONSTRAINTS IN A MULTIPLE PROJECT ENVIRONMENT

Review the triple constraints, which are part of every project: time, budget, and performance criteria. You noted that the constraints are then ranked in a special order: 1) driver, 2) middle constraint, and, 3) weak constraint.

The driver is the constraint so overwhelmingly important that if you fail to meet it, the project is a failure, no matter how well you meet the remaining constraints. If Noah's ark is not ready when the rain comes, explaining that Noah got the lumber at a bargain price is not likely to be counted as an excuse.

The weak constraint has the most flexibility, and this flexibility provides a tool to help you meet the driver.

Because of our basic concepts that *project* = *task* and *portfolio* = *project*, you need to realize that the triple constraints apply at all levels of the project environment. There are triple constraints for the portfolio, for each project inside the portfolio, and for each task inside each project. There can be conflicts among the constraint levels, and they can be the source of some of your management problems.

Your first goal has to be to define the triple constraints at each level. In Patrick's case, he needs to make sure that he understands the primary mission of his department. Does the organization primarily want him to make money, and secondarily publish high-quality technical information? Does the organization primarily want him to make money, and secondarily offer a long list of publications? Does the organization primarily want him to be a publisher of high-quality technical information, and secondarily to make money?

Each scenario will, of course, change how Patrick should manage his portfolio, decide which projects to put in it, and measure how well he is doing. If Patrick does not determine his real purpose, based on the organization's overall goals, he can inadvertently lead his team into disaster—while believing he is doing the right thing.

RESOLVING CONFLICTS BETWEEN PROJECT DRIVERS AND PORTFOLIO DRIVERS

Difference between project and portfolio drivers. If a project and a task are the same, a portfolio and a project are also the same. But the driver of the portfolio is not automatically identical to the driver of the individual projects within the portfolio.

That seems impossible, but look further. On a project/task level, you might have a project with time as the driver. That would imply that time is the driver for each task in the project. What if a task is noncritical? If it has slack, then time is not the most restrictive constraint. Therefore, the driver of that task is different from the driver of the project.

The same thing can be true of your portfolio. You must develop the portfolio's triple constraints and analyze their ranking to determine driver/middle/weak constraint order. This allows you to prioritize the individual projects within the portfolio and make the right strategic decisions, such as how to allocate resources across your projects, in order to optimize the driver.

Conflicts between project manager goals and portfolio manager goals. One problem that may arise, as a result of these different drivers, is that one of your project managers may see her goals differently. At the portfolio level, the project may be a low priority, low payoff issue that should be handled quickly. The project manager may feel, however, that the project is her baby.

Because the individual project manager tends to see the work in terms of her own project, she may put more time, energy, and resources than warranted into the project goal. You may find the project manager fighting for additional resources, arguing for greater priority, or pushing for more time than you believe is appropriate.

First, you are responsible for overall priority, and you sometimes need to make decisions that are right for the portfolio but wrong for the project. You might find yourself faced with having to say something like:

> I know you want to make this the best book you ever published, but I do not think you will sell more than five hundred copies. Because some of our other books might sell fifty thousand copies, they are more important. I need you to finish this book quickly and not put any more resources into it, because you will not get the payoff from the investment. I want the "best book we ever published" to be one that will sell well and have a larger audience.

Expect the project manager to react emotionally to this. You all want to do quality work and have that work recognized. To be told our project has a low priority—even if that is the absolute truth—can be upsetting. As the portfolio manager, your reaction might be, "Gee, that is tough—now get back to work"; but you cannot afford to ignore the project manager's feelings in this situation.

First, you need the team member to keep a positive attitude so that she can be effective on the next project. Second, you need the team member to learn to better understand overall goals; that is unlikely if the team member is angry. Third, you need the team member to decide properly how to finish—or abandon—the current project.

Allow team members in this situation to express their negative emotions—to vent a little bit. Lead them through the process of figuring the next steps to take, and allow them a little time to mourn what their project might have been.

Deciding when to kill a project. Along with the decision to lower a project's priority comes the decision to kill a project completely. Recall the juggling act in Chapter 1 where all the spinning plates had the same value. In our multiple-project environment, this is not necessarily true.

Use the priority management system in Section 2 of this book to rank the individual projects in your portfolio. How does each project contribute to meeting the portfolio goals? The process of prioritizing may get you to drop some projects from the schedule even before they start.

You may put some marginal projects in your schedule because you have the resources available. If things go wrong, or if other projects that have a higher priority are added to your schedule, you may need to drop some of the marginal projects. This can lead to the emotional issues just described.

You may also find it frustrating to kill a marginal project after time, effort, and resources have been invested in it. Ask yourself if it is possible to salvage the work; maybe the project can be put on indefinite hold rather than killed outright; maybe some of the work can be reused in other projects. If you have a project manager who is frustrated and hurt by the project's demise, ask him to think of ways to salvage the work. He may have some viable ideas.

TECHNIQUES FOR MANAGING PRIORITIES AND WORKFLOW

Part of achieving success in a multiple project environment is designing your own personal control systems. Following are ideas that others have used successfully.

■ Build your own control systems. Use color-coding for project status reports. Try colored stick-on dots, tinted papers, red dots for priority issues, and other tricks. Put your project-tracking information in your personal organizer, and calendar your tasks. Use separate clipboards for each project. Keep a project journal/work diary.

■ Organize yourself. Clean your desk at the end of each day. Write a weekly to-do list. Do a Monday morning update. Build quiet/think time into your work schedule. Buy tools to manage the paper on your desk, and learn to use them.

- Set and maintain good priorities. Learn to distinguish between importance and urgency. Rank your assignments by 1) which generates the most profit for the organization, 2) which yields greatest payoff for your time, and, 3) letting your management decide when neither 1 nor 2 is compelling.

- Speak up. Learn to say no when you are overloaded or cannot afford to be distracted. When something happens that may jeopardize the project, let the affected people know early. Negotiate. Be assertive.

My Current Authority Issues

Take the time to write your answers to each question fully, using extra paper if needed. It is important to write your ideas, for you will see them more clearly and be able to use them more effectively. You need to face these issues honestly. As you identify areas of difficulty and concern, you can determine strategies to facilitate growth and improvement.

1. **How would your boss define your current official role in managing your project portfolio? Is your authority in writing (part of your job description or by formal memo) or informal?**

   _____

   _____

   _____

   _____

   _____

2. **What do you need in resources to accomplish your portfolio goals? What resources do you have? If there is a gap, what strategy should you follow?**

   _____

   _____

   _____

   _____

   _____

3. **What authority (if any) do you have to make or approve purchases, negotiate and approve contracts, or make other decisions that bind your organization legally or financially?**

   _____

   _____

   _____

   _____

   _____

4. Do you select your own team members? Are they selected for you? Or is there a hybrid selection process?

_____

_____

_____

_____

_____

5. Does each key member of your project team report to you in a formal sense? If not, what level of authority do you possess (ability to fire, reprimand, dismiss from team, and so on)? Do any members of your project team outrank you in the normal office hierarchy?

_____

_____

_____

_____

_____

6. Who is responsible for creation of the plan, approval of changes to the plan, maintenance of the plan, and the making of work assignments from the plan? If not you, where do you fit in?

_____

_____

_____

_____

_____

7. Do you have direct access to the ultimate customer(s) or client(s) for the projects in your portfolio, or do you have to go through intervening management (internal or external)? Are you accepted by the customer as a technical authority? Do you regularly attend top-level meetings impacting the project?

_____

_____

_____

_____

_____

8. At what point do you have to gain the approval of others higher in the organization to make portfolio-related decisions? Do you have enough respect and acceptance from higher authority for your recommendations to be seriously considered and usually accepted?

_____

_____

_____

_____

_____

9. List the key organizational players with concern for the projects in your portfolio. Are there people in power positions who have agendas (hidden or clear) that affect the project outcome, resources, priority, or methodology? If so, who and what are they?

_____

_____

_____

_____

_____

10. What is the relative priority of the projects in your portfolio compared to other projects and portfolios within the organization? How do other organizational priorities affect your project portfolio?

_____

_____

_____

_____

My Delegated Needs and Goals

1. How would I rate the current skill and ability level of the project managers on my team? Are they adequate for the job that is expected of them? If not, what steps can I take to develop the skills and abilities I need?

_____

_____

_____

_____

_____

2. What authority do my project managers need to accomplish their projects in a timely and effective manner? What types of decisions should they make on their own without the need to consult with me? What types of decisions should they make but check with me first? What types of decisions should they bring to me and let me decide?

_____

_____

_____

_____

_____

3. What personal or political goals or agendas do my project managers and key team members have? Do any of them conflict with my goals or agenda? If so, what should I do to deal with these conflicts?

_____

_____

_____

_____

4. How good is the current communication between the individual project managers on my team and me? Are we able to identify and resolve conflicts, deal with any personality issues, and reach consensus on project goals, deadlines, and budgets? If there are problems, what strategies can I follow to overcome them?

_____

_____

_____

_____

_____

5. How would I rate my personal skill in delegating and empowering team members to do the work? If my delegating skills and confidence levels are not up to my needs, what will I do to improve my skills in delegating and empowering?

_____

_____

_____

_____

_____

SECTION 4

Interdependent Project Portfolios

CHAPTER 8

Juggling the Interdependent Project Portfolio

"The move to the new computer center is the biggest single project I've ever managed," Sarah observes. "To make it even more difficult, it has to be accomplished while keeping all the other projects and activities of my department running smoothly. On top of everything, if this project doesn't go well, it could turn into a first-class disaster for the company ... not to mention my own career!

"I've been on projects like this before. They start off smoothly, all right, but then comes crunch time, right toward the end when everybody's pulling all-nighters and it's anybody's guess whether we'll make it or not. That's what worries me.

"On top of everything else, my entire collection of projects is really part of the overall move of the entire company! It could be worse. I could be in charge of everything. Still, I have to make sure that I coordinate my work so that it fits into the overall move schedule."

DEFINITIONS

An *interdependent project* is a project that is part of a portfolio of projects aimed at achieving a common outcome. Not only must the project goal be reached, but it also must be reached in a way that fits with the other projects in the portfolio to achieve the overall goal.

No-fail budgeting is the process of allocating total portfolio resources to each project in the portfolio so that each project has the minimum necessary resources to succeed. Once each project has the minimum resources, the project manager can use the remaining resources to increase total portfolio quality.

Total portfolio quality is the achievement of the overall portfolio goal, as opposed to the achievement of individual project goals within the portfolio. This concept helps you and your project managers remember that what is good for an individual project is not always what is good for the portfolio as a whole.

Crunch time is a common experience on major projects. The work all seems to go perfectly until the very end, when suddenly everyone must work around the clock to cope with unanticipated disasters.

ABOUT INTERDEPENDENT PROJECT PORTFOLIOS

Projects in an interdependent project portfolio often vary dramatically in subject matter. In Sarah's case, her projects range from managing a physical move to purchasing new hardware, developing strategic documents, and developing computer programs, all aimed at the common outcome of making the move happen.

Who has expertise in every single one of these areas? Very few, indeed. When you manage an interdependent project portfolio, you can expect to be stretched professionally into new fields. You need to be an outstanding delegator, able to find and motivate professionals with the skills and experience you do not have.

Sarah's situation, as with Patrick's and Carolyn's, also involves the reality that projects take place inside organizations. She has regular management duties, meetings to attend, special assignments, and other elements of work. So does her staff.

Part of her situation—and one common to most interdependent project portfolios—is that she is responsible for ongoing work and projects while trying to fit this major additional function into her schedule. As a result, and similar to Patrick's situation, you need to remember that the techniques in this situation, once again, are in addition to, not instead of, the techniques for managing the independent project portfolio, as well as the task-oriented project portfolio.

Interdependent project portfolios tend to be long term and substantial in size, scope, and complexity. Individual projects in the portfolio may be of any size, from small and easy to huge and cumbersome.

You can also be in the situation of managing an interdependent project portfolio from the inside. While Sarah's situation is complex enough to be called an interdependent portfolio on its own, her portfolio can also be considered a project in an even larger interdependent portfolio consisting of the entire company move!

Notice that this reality adds a series of issues and problems for Sarah. She cannot just pick a time for the move, based on the convenience of her own department; she must coordinate her move with the corporate move. Otherwise, the loading dock might be in use, or the build-out of her space might conflict with other important priorities.

When managing a project within an interdependent portfolio, no matter how complex your issues are, you must remember that you can only succeed if your outcome dovetails with the other elements of the portfolio. Make sure you always keep your eye on the big picture.

INDEPENDENT PORTFOLIO MANAGEMENT VERSUS INTERDEPENDENT PORTFOLIO MANAGEMENT

As with the independent project portfolio, your interdependent project portfolio can benefit if you use the techniques of professional project management. In Section 3, you learned about both Gantt and PERT charting. Because independent projects are *independent,* the Gantt chart is an ideal way to display and understand them. Because interdependent projects require more attention to the idea of connectedness, you will find that in most cases the PERT chart is a more useful tool for understanding and control.

Again, keep in mind the key concept—

$$Project = Task$$

—to allow managing multiple projects using the techniques of single project management.

Another difference between the two types of portfolios is that failure is not allowed. If Patrick's schedule becomes unmanageable, he can let a project of lower priority slip—or cancel it altogether. Sarah does not have that option, at least not in her core projects. She must use the concept of *no-fail budgeting* to ensure that her resources are allocated to achieve every single project in the portfolio—at least to a minimally acceptable level of quality. She can use remaining resources to increase *total portfolio quality*, but she needs to be aware that increasing the quality of one project in the portfolio does not automatically increase total portfolio quality.

THE IRONY OF INTERDEPENDENT PROJECT PORTFOLIOS

Sarah's computer-center portfolio has another special issue in it—one that is common to interdependent project portfolios. The issue is this: *she has never done this before.* Although she is an experienced data processing manager, this particular situation has never occurred. In fact, there are many outstanding and experienced professionals in this field who have never had to move a computer center. Plus, Sarah is unlikely ever to move another computer center—and if she does, she will not move very many in an entire career.

There is an irony in interdependent project portfolios: the project manager and the team have probably never done this before. That is true even with some major projects.

The Smithsonian National Air and Space Museum, a $30 million federal project that opened in 1976 (ahead of schedule and under budget, by the way), was managed by Mike Collins, then director of the museum. Collins, best known as the Apollo 11 command module pilot, had never built a museum. Neither had his senior staff. The team did it anyway.

World War II Allied Commander General Dwight D. Eisenhower had never managed an international military alliance to coordinate a continental invasion before D-Day. He did it anyway.

Imagine the pastor of a church that decides to expand into a new building. Like Sarah and her computer center, the pastor may never have done it. If the pastor has, it will not have been very often. Yet, church building projects happen all the time. They do it anyway.

When you are put in charge of an interdependent project portfolio, and if you say to yourself, "I have no idea what I am doing because I have never done this before," relax, you are in good company. Just do it anyway.

CHAPTER 9

Planning an Interdependent Project Portfolio

Sarah would have preferred more notice, but the overall decision to move into a new building has already been made, the plans are in progress, and the deadline is set. She can't do much about it.

Her goals in planning are as follows.

■ *Make sure the physical move happens on schedule without any data loss. (This includes ensuring that backups are completed and protected.)*

■ *Make sure new equipment is installed, tested, and operational by the deadline.*

■ *Keep critical department functions operating during the move.*

■ *Avoid crunch time as much as humanly possible.*

DEFINITIONS

Here are the key terms you need in this chapter.

The *control point identification chart* is a tool for identifying problems to allow for early solution.

Finish-to-finish dependency describes a situation when the finish of task B is dependent upon the finish of task A. (It can start earlier.)

Frontloading is a strategy for doing as much of the project as you can up front. This builds in additional margin if things go wrong as you approach the deadline.

Lag time is extra time built into a project at the end to allow time to respond to emergencies. Unlike a lag activity, this time is not associated with any task; it can be used freely to respond to any emergencies.

Overlap dependency means the start of task B can begin sometime after the start of task A, but before task A finishes.

Start-to-start dependency is when the start of task B depends upon the start of task A. In a normal finish-to-start dependency, the start of task B depends on the finish of task A.

Task slack belongs to a single task, allowing it to be delayed without affecting the next task.

Path slack is slack that is shared among a sequence of tasks.

Free slack is the amount of time a task can be delayed before affecting the next task in the sequence.

Total slack is the amount of time a task can be delayed before affecting the deadline of the project.

PLANNING FOR INTERDEPENDENT PROJECT PORTFOLIOS

The process for planning the interdependent project portfolio is the same as that for the independent project portfolio.

Step 1: Define the Portfolio Goals

Make sure that you have a clear understanding of the portfolio goal and that you have prepared the objective in triple-constraint terms. You then need to determine the triple constraints for each of the projects in your portfolio—it is not necessarily the case that they will be the same.

In Sarah's case, the goal is to have a successful move without losing data or production time. The triple constraints are as follows.

■ Time: The move-in week has been scheduled for the week of September 22. All activities needed for the move-in must be ready by then. (Certain activities may take place after the move-in week, such as unpacking.)

■ Performance: Critical computer services are not interrupted, data is not lost, new equipment is installed and operational, and the staff is trained.

■ Budget: There is a fixed budget for new equipment ($1 million), and the overall move budget is $150,000.

Put the triple constraints in order. You can determine them by looking at the consequences of failure. The weak constraint is pretty obviously budget, since the damage done by going over budget is less than the damage done by missing the move-in or losing data and critical services.

Performance is probably the driver, because missing the move-in date, although costly and embarrassing, would be less serious than failing to deliver critical services or losing data. That gives us:

- driver: performance
- middle: time
- weak: budget.

Remember, when you determine the triple constraints, you often look at the consequences of failure. This does not mean that you intend to fail or want to fail. In fact, you want to achieve all three constraints. You need to understand the order of the constraints so you can make good decisions in the event of unforeseen difficulties.

Step 2: Prepare a Work Breakdown Structure

This portfolio consists of four interrelated projects: 1) the physical move, 2) new equipment procurement, 3) continuing operations and transition management, and, 4) new center implementation (training, documenting, dry run, debugging) (see Figure 9.1). Those projects become level 2 of the work breakdown structure (WBS). Each project consists of one or more tasks, which go in level 3 of the WBS. Some tasks may be large and complex enough to be considered projects of their own; you may break them down further into levels of the WBS.

Use the WBS to plan the management of your project. First, you need to assign a manager to each of the projects in the portfolio.

Tip! Let the managers help you plan. This not only lowers the amount of work you have to do but also helps them get buy-in and acceptance of the workload.

Verify triple constraints of each project. For example, the physical-move project is time driven, but continuing operations is performance driven. New equipment may be performance driven, but it could be budget driven, depending on the organizational issues that affect your decisions.

Remember that individual project managers on your team manage their projects according to their goals. Your job is to ensure that their work fits into your overall strategy.

Step 3: Conduct the Task Analysis Process

When you analyze tasks at the level of an interdependent project portfolio, you need to think of it as an entire process, rather than just filling out forms. An enormous amount of strategic and tactical thinking takes place, and this is one of your chief opportunities to get the members of your senior project team properly oriented, and prepare them to get results.

Determine available resources. One of the frequent situations in managing an interdependent project portfolio is that the portfolio comes on top of a normal load of projects and work. Using the techniques in Section 1, you and your team need to determine what time you can realistically commit to the portfolio's projects. This often means making decisions about what functions can be delayed until after completion of the portfolio. Delay everything that can be delayed, so you will have maximum time to accomplish what cannot be delayed.

Assign clear responsibilities. It is easy for important matters to slip in a project situation like this. People can easily get wrapped up in day-to-day activities. As the cartoon

Planning an Interdependent Project Portfolio

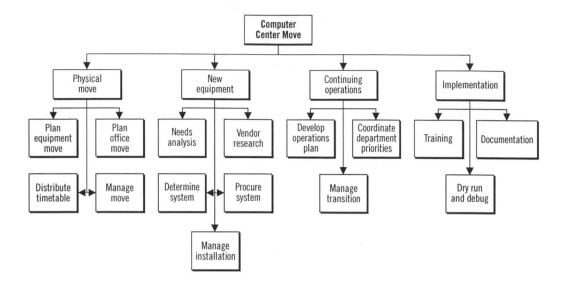

Figure 9.1 Work Breakdown Structure for Moving Computer Center to New Location

says, "When you are up to your rear end in alligators, it is hard to remind yourself that your original objective was to drain the swamp."

To overcome this, make sure that each activity is in the hands of a specific person or team and that accountability and authority have been clearly defined.

Determine good enough. While each individual project in the interdependent portfolio has to be accomplished, the quality standards vary. Because individual project managers tend to maximize their projects without regard for the portfolio as a whole, one of your key jobs is to establish *minimum* and *maximum* performance standards for each project. It is best to do this as a team activity—to get buy-in from the project managers.

Why maximum standards? Each project takes resources from the total pool. If a project is satisfactory at a certain level and exceeding that level takes more resources, is the improvement worth the cost? You must determine this by contribution to total portfolio quality.

Brainstorm effective strategies. Use your team resources to do some extensive brainstorming when faced with an interdependent project portfolio. Look for ways to save time, improve quality, and lower cost. Look for ways to reinvent methods of doing the individual projects.

Determine ways to monitor progress. You will need a regular schedule of meetings and reports to stay on top of the process. Plan them in advance, and be sure to follow good meeting practice, such as always having an agenda.

One good tactic to both monitor and motivate progress is to make a wall chart. Take one large, empty wall and display PERT and Gantt charts on it. Mark all progress issues on the charts so that they are constantly in view of all staff.

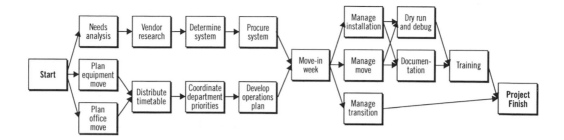

Figure 9.2 A PERT Chart Showing the Sequence of Tasks Involved in the Computer Move

Motivate early action. On any portfolio of this size and complexity, one key tactic is to get started early. While *crunch time* may be inevitable, you can at least minimize it if people start early.

Step 4: Prepare a PERT Chart for the Portfolio

Place the tasks from the WBS into a PERT-chart sequence. You inserted two milestones: Start and Project Finish. As with all milestones, they will have a time estimate of zero. They help organize your chart. One task, Move-in week, is a must-start activity; it is already scheduled and you need to work around it. Most tasks have to be done in time for the move-in; the move-in tasks are done during the move-in (they have a start-to-start dependency relationship).

Remember, the decisions you make in laying out your PERT chart are strategic decisions that affect your project. One of Sarah's most important goals is to minimize the crunch time on this project. She followed two strategies in laying out her PERT chart.

1. Frontloading: The more of this project you can get out of the way before the move-in date approaches, the better off you are. When managing a deadline-sensitive project with the possibility of unforeseen complications, put as much as possible up front.

2. Build in lag: Schedule the project to allow as much free time as possible between the end of the tasks immediately preceding the move-in week and the move-in week itself. Internal lag time lowers risk and increases safety.

Step 5: Determine the Critical Path

Place time estimates on your PERT chart, and determine the longest (critical) path. Identify available slack time. Slack time has several benefits.

First, slack is a way to lower risk. If you use the optional PERT time-estimating formula and calculate sigma (σ) for the paths, try to have 2σ of slack and lag available. This gives you a base 95 percent chance of reaching the deadline on time. If 2σ is unrealistic, take all you can get.

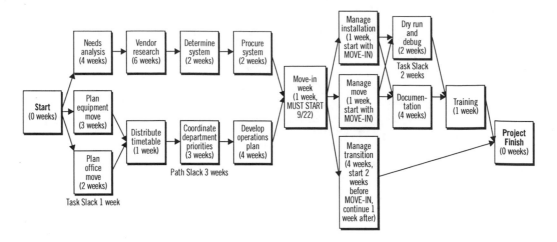

Figure 9.3 PERT Chart for Computer Move Showing Task Slack

Second, slack sometimes gives you the opportunity to optimize resources. If you have paths with excessive slack (more than 2σ), look to see if you can reassign people and resources from tasks on that path to critical tasks. The noncritical tasks take longer, but that is okay as long as you still have slack. The critical tasks go faster, which improves your total project performance.

Our computer-center PERT chart contains some special situations that might affect your planning (see Figure 9.3).

Task slack versus path slack. The task, Plan office move, contains one week of task slack. That means it can finish one week late without delaying the start of the next task or the end of the project. (This is also called free slack.) The entire task sequence from Plan equipment move through Develop operations plan (see Figure 9.3) is scheduled to take eleven weeks. The corresponding critical-path section (Needs analysis through Procure system) takes fourteen weeks. The difference, three weeks, is slack time.

Unlike the task slack situation, this three-week period belongs equally to all tasks. If Plan equipment move is late one week, it delays the start of Distribute timetable, which delays the start of Coordinate department priorities, which delays the start of Develop operations plan, but it does not delay the start of move-in week! In other words, all the tasks in that sequence can be a total of three weeks late (in any combination) before affecting the start of the next task.

The three weeks in this case are also called total slack. Plan equipment move has three weeks of total slack, which is how late it can be without affecting the critical path. It has no free slack because any delay in that task delays the start of the next task in the path. Develop operations plan has the same three weeks of total slack but also has three weeks of free slack—assuming all its predecessors finish on time!

Internal lag. Move-in week is a must-start activity (fixed in time, rather than just following its predecessor task), but that does not automatically mean that the project start date is fixed. Working backward from the move-in week task, the critical path is

The Juggler's Guide to Managing Multiple Projects

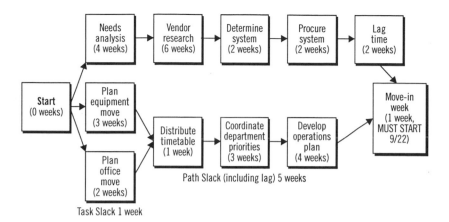

Figure 9.4 PERT Chart Showing Lag Times as an Activity

fourteen weeks to that point, which means that the project portfolio must start no later than the week of 6/16 to make the 9/22 deadline. However, this assumes that everything will go perfectly. A better strategy is to move the start date back. If you add two weeks of lag time to the critical path, backing the start date up to 6/2, you add that margin of safety to the portfolio (also lowering the crunch-time problem).

Figure 9.4 shows lag time as an activity. This is always a legitimate option, but it is not strictly necessary. Do it if it helps you keep better track of your project.

Step 6: Prepare a Gantt Chart for Calendar Management

In managing an interdependent portfolio, you should put greater emphasis on the PERT chart, because it does a much better job showing connections among the projects that make up the portfolio. As you mentioned, displaying a wall-sized PERT chart can be a powerful tool to help keep people focused on the goal.

A Gantt chart, however, does provide advantages in any time-sensitive project, because it shows the activities in a calendar form. There is no reason you must limit yourself to only one project view, especially if you are using project management software. Creating a Gantt chart from a PERT chart (or vice versa) is simply a matter of selecting the option from the menu and hitting Print.

In this chart, you chose not to show the lag as a separate activity; that is why there are no critical tasks in the project until you reach the move itself. Even the tasks you previously designated as *critical* can be late up to two weeks before they jeopardize the start of the move.

As in the independent project portfolio, you can use the Gantt chart as a way to monitor progress in calendar terms. You should also update the PERT chart to see progress in terms of dependency relationships.

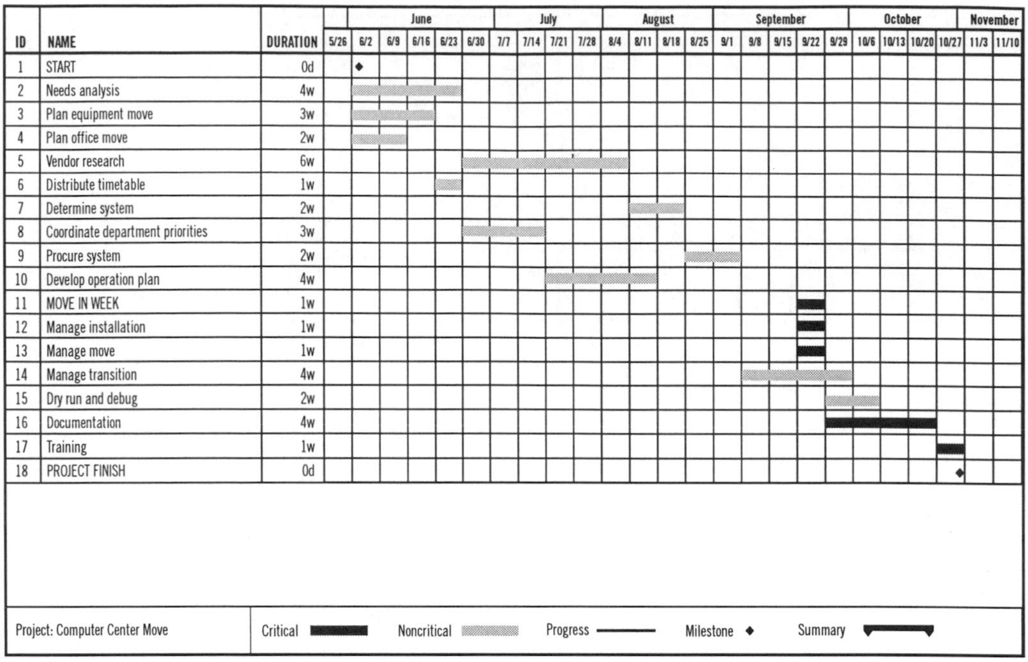
June
July
August
September
October
November
ID
NAME
DURATION
5/26
6/2
6/9
6/16
6/23
6/30
7/7
7/14
7/21
7/28
8/4
8/11
8/18
8/25
9/1
9/8
9/15
9/22
9/29
10/6
10/13
10/20
10/27
11/3
11/10
1 START 0d
2 Needs analysis 4w
3 Plan equipment move 3w
4 Plan office move 2w
5 Vendor research 6w
6 Distribute timetable 1w
7 Determine system 2w
8 Coordinate department priorities 3w
9 Procure system 2w
10 Develop operation plan 4w
11 MOVE IN WEEK 1w
12 Manage installation 1w
13 Manage move 1w
14 Manage transition 4w
15 Dry run and debug 2w
16 Documentation 4w
17 Training 1w
18 PROJECT FINISH 0d
Project: Computer Center Move
Critical
Noncritical
Progress
Milestone
Summary

Figure 9.5 Gantt Chart for Computer Center Move

Step 7: Prepare a Control Point Identification Chart for Critical, High-Risk Activities

The control point identification chart is a tool to help you identify something that might go wrong—or right—that would be out of the ordinary. Use a brainstorming session for each project in your portfolio to identify potential problems and opportunities. Then, identify early warning points, and list possible solutions and strategies.

While the planning issues for the interdependent project portfolio are similar to those of other projects, it is important that you adjust your perspective to the special issues that make this type of project different. By taking into account the differences in size and internal relationships, you will be well on the way to success.

Project/Task	What could go right/wrong?	How/when would I know?	What would I do?

Figure 9.6   Control Point Identification Chart

Analyzing Your Interdependent Portfolio

To manage your own interdependent project portfolio successfully, it is important that you start with the right focus. Make sure you know the answers to the following questions.

1. **Describe the interdependent project portfolio that you have to manage. What is the ultimate outcome, and how will you measure when you have achieved it?**

   _____

   _____

   _____

   _____

   _____

2. **What are the triple constraints of the portfolio, and how are they ranked in terms of priority?**

   _____

   _____

   _____

   _____

   _____

3. **What resources do you have available (people, equipment, money)? How can you obtain additional resources if required? How can you use the flexibility in the weak constraint to help you meet your goals?**

   _____

   _____

   _____

   _____

4. What skills, knowledge, and experience are needed in your team to accomplish your objective? What skills do you have? What skills can your team members supply? What skills, knowledge, and experience are missing? How will you get them?

_____

_____

_____

_____

_____

5. What political/organizational issues could affect your portfolio performance? What potential conflicts can you anticipate from team members and subordinate project managers? How do different people see your goal?

_____

_____

_____

_____

_____

CHAPTER 10

How to Manage Multiple Projects in an Interdependent Portfolio

"Making a good plan and thinking about strategic issues is obviously important," Sarah observes. *"I still wonder about the actual management, however. What if things don't go as expected? What about outside pressures? Will my team stay motivated? In other words, how do I manage the portfolio and achieve the goal?"*

Sarah's concerns include:

■ *How can I keep my team focused on the goal without either panicking or getting distracted?*

■ *How can I make sure my team chooses the right balance between ongoing work and this important move?*

■ *How can I keep crunch time from becoming a disaster?*

As with our other project portfolios, the management phase is different from the planning phase. Take a look at the special issues involved in managing a successful interdependent project portfolio.

DEFINITIONS

Here are the key terms you will need to know in this chapter.

An *esclating objective* is a project situation in which the agreed-upon objective grows during the process (also called *mission creep*).

A *change order* is a change in the project objective requested by the customer (internal or external).

The *Godzilla principle* states that if you catch a problem early, it is easier to solve.

The *pop-up principle* states that when you solve a problem, the solution itself usually contains a problem.

THE ART OF MANAGING THE INTERDEPENDENT PORTFOLIO

The process for managing multiple projects is additive: you need to do all the elements of managing the task-oriented portfolio and the independent portfolio, and then add the special features of the interdependent portfolio on top of them.

The interdependent project portfolio is defined as a large project with major divisions important enough to be considered projects in their own right. The first key to managing this type of portfolio is not to allow any individual project to fail without fundamentally compromising the success of the portfolio.

The Smithsonian National Air and Space Museum was both a large project and an interdependent project portfolio. Each individual exhibit gallery clearly qualified as a project; each aircraft restored was a project; the construction of the building itself was a project. The failure of any project within the portfolio would compromise and possibly destroy the success of the entire portfolio. For example, if all the exhibit galleries had been successfully completed, but the building construction had been delayed, the museum would not have opened on time. Essentially, the quality of the galleries would have been irrelevant if there had been no building in which to put them.

As Ed Harris said in the movie, *Apollo 13*, "Failure is not an option."

YOUR ROLE AS PORTFOLIO MANAGER

From a management point of view, one of your critical responsibilities is to help your individual project managers stay focused on the goal. It is all too easy to become distracted by the individual requirements of a project within the portfolio and pursue them in a way that is detrimental to the interests of the portfolio as a whole.

What is best for an individual project in the portfolio is not necessarily best for the portfolio itself. For example, in the portfolio involving the computer center move, there is an obvious conflict between Manage transition and Manage installation. The manager of the transition has primary responsibility for ensuring that critical functions run smoothly. The manager of the installation has primary responsibility for ensuring that the installation is successful. There are numerous steps that each manager may take to make his job easier—at the expense of making the other manager's job more difficult.

Maximizing either project at the expense of the other can be damaging to the portfolio as a whole. If you make the transition run perfectly by interfering with the installation, you may have a late and trouble-filled installation. If you make the installation run perfectly by interfering with the transition, you may fail to keep up with critical ongoing functions.

The right approach strikes a happy medium. Neither project manager gets everything she might want in order to make individual projects perfect. How do you reach a perfect balance? Following are some management suggestions.

■ Face conflict early. Search your plan for potential conflicts, and have a meeting with the affected project managers. Ask them to participate in identifying the right balance and the compromises each must make to achieve the goal.

■ Set up coordination systems. Have the project managers meet regularly (with or without you) to work out strategies and agreements on potential conflict areas. Hold them accountable for working together smoothly.

■ Make decisions as needed. One key responsibility of the portfolio manager is to resolve areas of conflict when individual project managers cannot. Perhaps there is a policy issue at stake. Perhaps one project has to suffer much more than another does. Perhaps both performance objectives cannot be met at the same time, and something has to give. Those decisions are yours. Make them clearly.

■ Be alert to politics. Do not be surprised if one, or both, of the affected project managers decides to use a strategic approach to get what she wants. It is the job, after all, of a project manager to achieve the project goal, and political maneuvering is one way to attain it. It is not necessary to punish someone for being political, but ensure that you make firm decisions and justify them in terms of portfolio needs.

No-Fail Budgeting in the Interdependent Portfolio

Another key management issue in the interdependent project portfolio is resource allocation. Given the reality that resources are always limited and opportunity is unlimited, you must allocate the available resources to the projects in your portfolio. To ensure that you meet your most important objectives, you should allocate resources in a two-pass process.

First, identify the minimum acceptable performance level for each project in the portfolio and the resources necessary to achieve that minimum level. This is called *no-fail budgeting*. Allocate the minimum resources. If you have no more resources, the minimum is now the best you can do.

Second, allocate any remaining resources to achieve maximum portfolio achievement. Do not allocate resources evenly across your projects, because some of your projects do not improve portfolio quality once they have achieved the minimum.

For example, in construction, no one paints the inside of the drywall, because it does not add to the quality of the building as a whole.

COPING WITH THE ESCALATING OBJECTIVE

While certain management problems can affect any manager in any situation at any time, one particular nightmare for the project portfolio manager is the circumstance of *escalating project objectives*. This occurs when the initial project objective, although properly approved, starts creeping upward as the project progresses. Time compresses, budget shrinks, and performance criteria increase.

Changes in projects lead to *change orders*. Whether change orders are formal or informal, they tend to be common to project management experience. You must learn how to cope with the change.

Try the following techniques, especially at the beginning of your project.

■ Do the entire triple constraints process. This may be the source of some problems if you have not fully negotiated and explored the triple constraints. Too many project portfolio managers neglect identifying the underlying project reason and the management, organizational, and customer issues that influence it.

■ Identify the players. As part of the triple constraints process, remember that a project has a central objective and often secondary objectives that are the related interests of all those who form the project constituency. You must discover who your project constituency is, interview him, learn his goals and perceptions, and integrate as many of those goals as possible without compromising the central objective. Do not forget personal as well as external motivations.

■ Put it in writing, and shop it around. A good goal is a written goal. Make sure people know the goal in advance and in writing and have an early opportunity to challenge that goal. Although it can be difficult to negotiate a workable compromise, it is much easier than coping with a late-project major change order that virtually guarantees disaster. Although people can change a written goal, it is harder than changing an unwritten goal. As a famous Hollywood mogul said, "An oral contract is worth the paper it's printed on."

■ Show others your plans, schedules, and budgets. You cannot assume that others in management will understand the consequences of a proposed project change as well as you do. Document the consequences of a change clearly and objectively. When a change is requested, print out a current plan and budget. Next, integrate the change into the existing schedule, and print out the revised plan and budget. Third, brainstorm the most proactive ways of achieving the new goal. Revise the schedule and budget to accommodate the change. Print that out. Now, go to management or the customer. Show them the three versions: 1) no change, 2) integrate the change and proceed, and, 3) best ideas to integrate the change while achieving the time, budget, and performance goals. Ask for suggestions. You may still have to make the change, but you may better negotiate the corresponding changes in time, budget, and performance.

■ Build change into the process. In many projects, the nature of the work makes change orders inevitable. It may not be possible to identify all the real needs until the work has progressed to a certain point. In this case, you need to schedule change in the process. Set milestones in your project schedule for customer review and expectation development, tasks for integration of requirements changes, and redevelopment to accommodate changes. Build this into your initial schedule and budget. If it is inevitable, plan for it.

PROBLEM-SOLVING STRATEGIES

The first—and still the best—problem-solving strategy is to avoid the problem. Effective planning, including the control point identification chart, reduces both the number and the severity of project problems.

Here are a few additional pointers to help you in solving problems.

The Godzilla principle. In Japanese monster movies, there is frequently a scene where the monster du jour (Godzilla, Mothra, Gamora, and so on) is a cute baby monster. People say, "Oh, what a cute little monster!" Obviously, no urgency exists. They ignore the monster.

They wait until the monster is full-grown and busily stomping downtown Tokyo, then they shout, "What are we going to do?" The answer is, of course, nothing. When Godzilla is rampaging through downtown Tokyo, there is very little you can do about it. The best option is past.

On your projects, spend time on baby-monster patrol. Every time you find a little problem with the power to later grow into a big one, stomp on it at once.

There are three opportunities when problem solving is possible: 1) when you first think of it, 2) when you first detect it, and, 3) when it actually happens. The rule of problem solving is, the closer you get to the problem, the fewer the options available to solve the problem.

If you are planning a summer picnic, and rain is a possibility, you can schedule a rain date. You have solved the problem at the moment you thought of it.

Perhaps you missed that opportunity, but you heard a weather report forecasting rain a few days before the picnic. It is too late to recall the invitations and set up a rain date, so you rent a tent, increasing the cost. At least people will be dry. You have solved the problem when you first detected it.

Perhaps you do not watch the news, and you missed the weather report. You wake up the morning of the picnic, and it is raining cats and dogs. Now you are madly scrambling for umbrellas, changing activities, and trying to keep the picnic from becoming a complete muddy ruin. You have solved the problem when it happens.

While you cannot anticipate everything or solve every problem, you can improve your problem-solving effectiveness by using this strategy.

Pop-up principle. Every time you solve a problem, something else pops up.

Schedule a rain date for the picnic? New problems pop up, such as extra time, effort, and cost to book the site for a rain date—loss of perishable food and some loss of available guests on the second date.

Rent a tent? New problems occur: additional costs and activity cancellation.

Pop-ups do not invalidate a problem-solving strategy; they present one more challenge to overcome. When you come up with a solution to a problem, ask yourself, "What are the pop-ups? What negative consequences can arise from this solution?" Sometimes, the negative consequences are minor, even insignificant. In that case, you can ignore the pop-up. Sometimes, the cure is worse than the disease. If the solution is worse than living with the problem, do not choose that particular solution. Sometimes, the negative consequences of the pop-up can be minimized. Look for ways to adjust the solution. Of course, this can create another pop-up!

Use the triple constraints. Every problem affects one or more of the triple constraints; that is what makes it a problem. A problem may be one of the following four types.

1. Time problem: Tasks take longer than expected.
2. Budget problem. Tasks cost more than expected.
3. Performance problem. Tasks are not delivering the expected result.
4. Resource problem. Resources are not available to do the work—this causes problems in one or more of the constraints.

Because the triple constraints are always in priority order, the seriousness of a problem depends on which constraint is affected. If a problem affects the driver, it is very serious and must be solved. If a problem affects the weak constraint, it may not be worth the effort required to solve it.

For the picnic, imagine you are thinking about renting a tent. If budget is the driver, the tent may cost too much. It is not an acceptable solution. If budget is the weak constraint, the extra cost may be irrelevant. Use the order of the constraints to determine the seriousness of problems, and use the flexibility in the weak constraint as a tool to help you solve them.

A Final Word about Managing Multiple Projects

The futurist Alvin Toffler predicted that the concept of bureaucracy would give way to a new organizational strategy, the *ad-hocracy*. He might have been talking about project managers of single and multiple projects.

As a project manager, you traditionally have more responsibility than authority. In fact, you are often in a situation when you need the willing and voluntary cooperation of people over whom you have no authority if you are to achieve your goals. You do this through persuasion, negotiation, planning, communication, and professionalism. You do this by developing your skills and knowledge. You do this by using the tools of project management and fitting them to the circumstances of your organization and your work.

When you do, you will find yourself fitting the traditional definition of a project manager:

> People responsible for doing something that has never been done before, for people who don't know what they want, who must first predict the unknown, make a plan to cope with the unforeseen, and execute the plan with too-limited resources that they do not control, and who are held completely responsible for the results, even if miracles are required.

You can do it. Good luck.

BIBLIOGRAPHY

Baker, Sunny and Kim Baker. 1992. *On Time-On Budget: A Step by Step Guide for Managing Any Project*. New York: Prentice Hall

Caroselli, Marlene. 1992. *Meetings That Work*. Mission, Kansas: SkillPath Publications, Inc.

Cleland, David I. and William R. King. 1983. *Project Management Handbook*. New York: Van Nostrand Reinhold Company.

Dobson, Michael. 1996. *Practical Project Management*. Mission, Kansas: SkillPath Publications.

Frame, J. Davidson. 1989. *Managing Projects in Organizations*. San Francisco: Jossey-Bass, Inc. Publishers.

Gardner, Reich. 1989. *How to Manage Projects* Audiotape. Mission, Kansas: SkillPath Publications, Inc.

Gonick, Larry and Woolcott Smith. 1993. *The Cartoon Guide to Statistics*. New York: HarperCollins Publishers.

Gray, Clifford F. 1981. *Essentials of Project Management*. New York: Petrocelli Books, Inc.

Haynes, Marion E. 1981. *Project Management*. Los Altos, California: Crisp Publications, Inc.

Imai, Masaaki. 1986. *Kaizen: The Key to Japan's Competitive Success*. New York: McGraw-Hill Publishing Company.

Kennedy, Marilyn Moates. 1989. *Office Politics* Audiotape. Chicago, Illinois: Nightingale-Conant Corporation.

Lowery, Gwen. 1992. *Managing Projects with Microsoft Project*. New York: Van Nostrand Reinhold Company.

Temme, Jim. 1990. *Managing Multiple Projects, Priorities and Deadlines* Audiotape. Mission, Kansas: SkillPath Publications, Inc.

———. 1993. *Productivity Power*. Mission, Kansas: SkillPath Publications, Inc.

Towers, Mark. 1993. *Dynamic Delegation*. Mission, Kansas: SkillPath Publications, Inc.

Zinn, Dain. 1994. *Project Management* Audiotape. Chicago, Illinois: Nightingale-Conant Corporation.

Additional Resources

Project Management Institute, Inc., Four Campus Boulevard, Newtown Square, Pennsylvania 19073-3299, (610) 456-4600.

Software Sources. PC Warehouse (800) 367-7080 or MacWarehouse (800) 255-6227.

GLOSSARY

budget constraint

   The money or resources you can use to achieve the project goal. One of the triple constraints.

change order

   A change in the project objective requested by the customer (internal or external).

control point identification chart

   A tool for identifying problems to allow for early solution.

CPM chart

   A type of network planning chart.

cross-project resources

   The people and tools that accomplish the projects in an independent project portfolio. While the projects do not directly relate to each other, they draw on the same resources. If a resource is late on one project, that can affect the next project(s) on which the resource is scheduled.

crunch time

   The common experience on major projects that the work all seems to go perfectly until the very end, when suddenly everyone works around-the-clock to cope with unanticipated disasters.

dependent task

   A task whose start depends on the completion of one or more predecessor tasks.

driver

   The most important of the triple constraints for your project. The other constraints are ranked as middle and weak.

escalating objective

   A common project situation in which the agreed-upon objective grows during the process (also called mission creep).

finish-to-finish dependency

   The finish of task B is dependent on the finish of task A (it can start earlier).

free slack

   The amount of time a task can be delayed before affecting the next task in the sequence.

frontloading

The strategy of completing as much of the project as you can up front, which builds in additional margin if things go wrong as you approach the deadline.

Gantt chart

A timeline chart that shows the sequence of tasks in your project over a calendar period.

Godzilla principle

If you catch a problem early, it's easier to solve.

independent project

A project that is part of a portfolio of projects, usually similar in subject matter, whose success and failure is independent of other projects in the portfolio.

interdependent project

A project that is part of a portfolio of projects aimed at achieving a common outcome. Not only must the project goal be reached, but it must also be reached in a way that lets it fit with the other projects in the portfolio to achieve the overall goal.

lag activity

A task that requires you to allocate time, but no resources.

lag time

Lag time is extra time built into a project at the end to give you time to respond to emergencies. Unlike a lag activity, this time isn't associated with any task; it can be used freely to respond to any emergencies.

least resource

When you schedule multiple resources across multiple projects, you may not have the same quantity of each resource. The least resource is the resource of which you have the smallest available quantity.

leveling

Rearranging the schedule to eliminate resource overloads.

leveling within slack

Rearranging the schedule without letting the deadline slip.

middle constraint

The second-most important triple constraint for your project. See driver.

mission creep

See escalating objective.

network planning

The process of putting your tasks in the order you need to do them. You may put your tasks in a dependent or parallel sequence. The network diagram is also called a PERT chart or CPM chart.

no-fail budgeting

The process of allocating total portfolio resources to each project in the portfolio so that each project has the minimum necessary resources to succeed. Once each project has the minimum, the project manager can then use the remaining resources to increase total portfolio quality.

overlap dependency

The start of task B can begin sometime after the start of task A, but before Task A finishes.

parallel task

A task done in the same time frame as one or more other tasks.

path slack

Slack that is shared among a sequence of tasks.

performance criteria

What the project must do once it's complete. One of the triple constraints.

PERT chart

A type of network planning chart.

pop-up principle

When you solve a problem, the solution itself usually contains a problem.

portfolio

Our name for a collection of projects co-managed under the same management umbrella.

portfolio constraints

The triple constraints of the entire portfolio, as distinct from the constraints of the individual projects within the portfolio.

predecessor task

A task that must be done before another task (dependent) can begin.

project

A project is a specific work assignment outside the routine of the normal job that has a planned end and a measurable accomplishment to be achieved.

project management software

A software package that creates and calculates project management charts, such as Gantt, PERT, and CPM.

resource

People, tools, equipment, and money that you must assign and allocate to get the work done.

resource Gantt chart

A Gantt chart that shows how your resources are allocated.

resource overload

When you have more jobs than resources during some periods of your project.

resource planning

Determining how to get the best use of people, equipment, tools, and money to get the job done.

slack resource

A resource without a job during some periods of your project.

SMART goals

Acronym for Specific, Measurable, Agreed-Upon (or Accountable), Realistic, and Time-Specific. A standard method of deciding if your goals are properly drawn.

start-to-start dependency

The start of task B depends on the start of task A.

task analysis

the process of gathering together all the information you need to manage each task in your project. A great aid in delegating.

task slack

Slack that belongs to a single task, allowing it to be delayed without affecting the next task.

Task-oriented project portfolio

A portfolio of small projects, each of which consists of a small number of tasks. We treat each project in the portfolio as a single task to help us schedule and manage the work.

task

An assignment with a measurable goal—and limited time and resources available to accomplish it.

time constraint

The amount of time you have to complete the project and/or the project deadline. One of the triple constraints.

time-fixed projects

Projects that have a fixed deadline (time is always the driver).

time-variable projects

Projects with flexibility in their deadlines (either budget or performance criteria is the driver).

total portfolio quality

The achievement of the overall portfolio goal, as opposed to the achievement of individual project goals within the portfolio. This concept is to help you and your subordinate project managers remember that what is good for an individual project is not necessarily good for the portfolio as a whole.

total slack

The amount of time a task can be delayed before affecting the deadline of the project.

tracking Gantt chart

A Gantt chart that lets you compare the actual to the plan for your project tasks.

triple constraints

The three parts of a project definition. how much time you have, how much money or resources can you use, and what does it have to accomplish. Usually called time constraint, budget constraint, and performance criteria. They are usually prioritized in an order of driver, middle constraint, and weak constraint.

weak constraint

The most flexible of the triple constraints for your project.

work

The rest of the job that you must accomplish while juggling projects on top of it. Work has no planned end to it.

work breakdown structure (WBS)

A method for breaking your project into component tasks and organizing your management structure.

INDEX

U

urgency   16, 93, 121
    measuring   16
    addiction   16

W

work breakdown structure   34, 36–37, 107,
    109

worksheets   13, 17, 22, 23, 40
    planning your priorities   28
    project control   12, 14, 39
    project/goal planning   27
    task analysis   34, 39, 107

UPGRADE YOUR
PROJECT MANAGEMENT
KNOWLEDGE WITH
FIRST-CLASS
PUBLICATIONS FROM PMI

PROJECT MANAGEMENT SOFTWARE SURVEY

The PMI® *Project Management Software Survey* offers an efficient way to compare and contrast the capabilities of a wide variety of project management tools. More than two hundred software tools are listed with comprehensive information on systems features, how they perform time analysis, resource analysis, cost analysis, performance analysis, and cost reporting, and how they handle multiple projects, project tracking, charting, and much more. The survey is a valuable tool to help narrow the field when selecting the best project management tools.
ISBN: 1-880410-52-4 (paperback), ISBN: 1-880410-59-1 (CD-ROM)

SUCCESSFUL INFORMATION SYSTEM IMPLEMENTATION,
SECOND EDITION

Successful implementation of information systems technology lies in managing the behavioral and organizational components of the process. Past data on this subject has involved mostly case studies, but this book provides practical information those implementing information systems can use now. Pinto and Millet offer practical information on "approaching the subject from a managerial, rather than a technical, perspective." The second edition of this work covers such topics as implementation theory, prioritizing projects, implementation success and failure, critical success factors, and more!
ISBN: 1-880410-66-4

RECIPES FOR PROJECT SUCCESS

This book is destined to become "the" reference book for beginning project managers, particularly those who like to cook! Practical, logically developed project management concepts are offered in easily understood terms in a lighthearted manner. They are applied to the everyday task of cooking-from simple, single dishes, such as homemade tomato sauce for pasta, made from the bottom up, to increasingly complex dishes or meals for groups that in turn require an understanding of more complex project management terms and techniques. The transisition between cooking and project management discussions is smooth, and tidbits of information provided with the receipes are interesting and humorous.
ISBN: 1-880410-58-3 (paperback)

TOOLS AND TIPS FOR TODAY'S PROJECT MANAGER

This guide book is valuable for understanding project management and performing to quality standards. Includes project management concepts and terms—old and new—that are not only defined but also are expalined in much greater detail than you would find in a typical glossary. Also included are tips on handling such seemingly simple everyday tasks as how to say "No" and how to avoid telephone tag. It's a reference you'll want to keep close at hand.
ISBN: 1-880410-61-3 (paperback)

The Future of Project Management

The project management profession is going through tremendous change—both evolutionary and revolutionary. Some of these changes are internally driven while many are externally driven. Here, for the first time, is a composite view of some major trends occurring throughout the world and the implication of them on the profession of project management and on the Project Management Institute. Read the views of the 1998 PMI Research Program Team, a well-respected futurist firm and other authors. This book represents the beginning of a journey and through inputs from readers and others, it will continue as a work in progress.
ISBN: 1-880410-71-0 (paperback)

New Resources for PMP Candidates

The following publications are resources that certification candidates can use to gain information on project management theory, principles, techniques, and procedures.

PMP Resource Package

Earned Value Project Management
    by Quentin W. Fleming and Joel M. Koppelman
Effective Project Management: How to Plan, Manage, and Deliver Projects on Time and Within Budget
    by Robert K. Wysocki, et al.
A Guide to the Project Management Body of Knowledge (PMBOK™ Guide)
    by the PMI Standards Committee
Human Resource Skills for the Project Manager
    by Vijay K. Verma
The New Project Management
    by J. Davidson Frame
Organizing Projects for Success
    by Vijay K. Verma
Principles of Project Management
    by John Adams, et al.
Project & Program Risk Management
    by R. Max Wideman, Editor
Project Management Casebook
    edited by David I. Cleland, et al.
Project Management: A Managerial Approach, Third Edition
    by Jack R. Meredith and Samuel J. Mantel, Jr.
Project Management: A Systems Approach to Planning, Scheduling, and Controlling, Sixth Edition
    by Harold Kerzner

A Guide to the Project Management Body of Knowledge (PMBOK™ Guide)

The basic management reference for everyone who works on projects. Serves as a tool for learning about the generally accepted knowledge and practices of the profession. As "management by projects" becomes more and more a recommended business practice worldwide, the *PMBOK™ Guide* becomes an essential source of information that should be on every manager's bookshelf. Available in hardcover or paperback, the *PMBOK™ Guide* is an official standards document of the Project Management Institute.
ISBN: 1-880410-12-5 (paperback), ISBN: 1-880410-13-3 (hardcover)

INTERACTIVE PMBOK™ GUIDE

This CD-ROM makes it easy for you to access the valuable information in PMI's *PMBOK™ Guide*. Features hypertext links for easy reference—simply click on underlined words in the text, and the software will take you to that particular section in the *PMBOK™ Guide*. Minimum system requirements: 486 PC; 8MB RAM; 10MB free disk space; CD-ROM drive, mouse, or other pointing device; and Windows 3.1 or greater.

MANAGING PROJECTS STEP-BY-STEP™

Follow the steps, standards, and procedures used and proven by thousands of professional project managers and leading corporations. This interactive multimedia CD-ROM based on PMI's *PMBOK™ Guide* will enable you to customize, standardize, and distribute your project plan standards, procedures, and methodology across your entire organization. Multimedia illustrations using 3-D animations and audio make this perfect for both self-paced training or for use by a facilitator.

PMBOK™ Q&A

Use this handy pocket-sized question-and-answer study guide to learn more about the key themes and concepts presented in PMI's international standard, *PMBOK™ Guide*. More than 160 multiple-choice questions with answers (referenced to the *PMBOK™ Guide*) help you with the breadth of knowledge needed to understand key project management concepts.
ISBN: 1-880410-21-4 (paperback)

PMI PROCEEDINGS LIBRARY CD-ROM

This interactive guide to PMI's annual Seminars & Symposium proceedings offers a powerful new option to the traditional methods of document storage and retrieval, research, training, and technical writing. Contains complete paper presentations from PMI '92–PMI '97 with full-text search capability, convenient onscreen readability, and PC/Mac compatibility.

PMI PUBLICATIONS LIBRARY CD-ROM

Using state-of-the-art technology, PMI offers complete articles and information from its major publications on one CD-ROM, including *PM Network* (1990–97), *Project Management Journal* (1990–97), and *A Guide to the Project Management Body of Knowledge*. Offers full-text search capability and indexing by *PMBOK™ Guide* knowledge areas. Electronic indexing schemes and sophisticated search engines help to find and retrieve articles quickly that are relevant to your topic or research area.

Also Available from PMI

Project Management for Managers
Mihály Görög, Nigel J. Smith
ISBN: 1-880410-54-0 (paperback)

Project Leadership: From Theory to Practice
Jeffery K. Pinto, Peg Thoms, Jeffrey Trailer, Todd Palmer, Michele Govekar
ISBN: 1-880410-10-9 (paperback)

ORDER ONLINE AT
WWW.PMIBOOKSTORE.ORG

Book Ordering Information

Phone: 412.741.6206

Fax: 412.741.0609

Email: pmiorders@abdintl.com

Mail: PMI Publications Fulfillment Center,
    PO Box 1020,
    Sewickley, Pennsylvania 15143-1020 USA
